COMPLETE

cat

care

COMPLETE

cat
care

WHAT EVERY CAT LOVER NEEDS TO KNOW

Dr Bruce Fogle DVM MRCVS

MITCHELL BEAZLEY

For Macy

Complete Cat Care
Bruce Fogle DVM MRCVS

First published in 2011 by Mitchell Beazley,
an imprint of Octopus Publishing Group Ltd,
Endeavour House, 189 Shaftesbury Avenue, London, WC2 8JY
An Hachette UK Company
www.octopusbooks.co.uk

A CIP catalogue record for this book is available from the British Library.

ISBN: 978 1 84533 5441

Commissioning Editor Helen Griffin
Project Editor Georgina Atsiaris
Senior Art Editor Juliette Norsworthy
Designer Lizzie Ballantyne
Copy-Editor Candida Frith-Macdonald
Proofreader Elaine Koster
Picture Researcher Roland and Sara Smithies
Production Manager Peter Hunt
Indexer Diana Le Core

Colour reproduction in Singapore
Printed and bound in China

Jacket photography: front, Wojtek Kalinowski Photography/Corbis; back,
left to right, top to bottom, Friday; Mikhail Dudarev; Jerome Dillard;
AlexandrKalinkin; Daisy Garcia; jeancliclac; Frenk_Danielle Kaufmann;
Parrus; Philip Date; Natali; Eric Isselée, all Fotolia.com

Contents

Introduction

If you haven't ever lived with a cat I wouldn't be surprised if you wonder why those of us who do, do. "It may be pretty but why live with a selfish little thug?" you may ask. "Why share your home, and your emotions, with such an independent animal that always marches to its own tune?"

Of course, if you have ever lived with one, you already know that a cat is more than just the raw outdoors brought into your home, more than simply a window into the natural world. Cats may still be in transition from self-sufficiency to dependent domesticity, but they've travelled a long way – and never more so than in the last 50 years, as we learned just how important very early experiences are in forming the adult personality of what is now perhaps our most numerous animal companion.

Some of you know I've written other books about how the cat's mind works, about their history, variety, health, and nutrition. I guesstimated the world's total cat population at 200 million, but that was woefully wrong. The unowned or feral cat population is much larger than I thought. Scientists now estimate there are 600 million cats living throughout the world, most of which are feral. That makes the cat perhaps the most successful small, land predator living today.

The domestic cat evolved from the Near Eastern wildcat. Domestic cats that live in our homes are pets. Amongst pet cats, those that decide themselves who they mate with are the random-breds; those we selectively breed to conform to set standards are the pure-breds or pedigrees. Even in the most affluent environments, pure-breds make up only a tiny percentage of all pet cats. Cats that live in our towns and gardens, depending on us to put out food for them, are semi-feral while those that survive by finding their own food are truly feral. Of course, all of these cats are also random-bred, but the coat colours and sizes of these cats do vary according to what region of the world they live in. These cats are an enormous genetic bank that pet cats continue to come from.

What we somewhat belatedly learned in the latter half of the 20th century, simply through careful observation, was that if feral kittens are brought into our homes and handled intensively from three to seven weeks of age, they easily make the transition to domesticity. There are no genetic differences in tameness or tameability between feral and pet cats; the only difference is in their early upbringing. What we also learned was that for most cats, living with people, or with dogs for that matter, is easier than living with other cats that they were not raised with. But if kittens are denied routine human contact during those important first seven weeks of life, they will probably retain a prolonged timid fear of people. Repeated, early contact with humans is vital for a cat to develop a strong physical and emotional relationship with us.

In the first part of this book I'll briefly explain how a very small number of Near Eastern wildcats, perhaps as few as five of them, adapted to living in close proximity to people and "mothered" all of today's domestic cats, including the burgeoning number of new breeds. Today, the luckiest cats end up in homes with people who understand that they have to invest a little time up front to earn the extraordinarily wonderful rewards that come from living with an accommodating cat. I'll explain how cats communicate with each other and with us, and how we sometimes misinterpret what they are saying or doing because they are less gregariously sociable than we are. I'll also explain that if you understand how cats think, it becomes quite easy to train them. I'll show you step by step ways to do so. I've been a clinical veterinarian for over 40 years, so don't be surprised that the largest chapter in this book is on care, on maintaining good health. Cats may be superbly efficient predators, but they are also potential prey to larger predators, so they evolved behaviours to mask when they are unwell and vulnerable. I'll describe the sometimes subtle signs to look for when your cat is ailing. Medical conditions are almost always easier to treat when a diagnosis is made sooner rather than later.

During the time I've been a vet I've watched as the cat moved from the garden to the kitchen and now into our bedrooms! As they inveigled themselves more intimately into our lives,

the intensity of our relationship with them increased. After all, we're all suckers for the body rub, for the leap onto the lap, for that tranquil and comforting purr. These are natural kitten or cat activities that we've intentionally perpetuated into adulthood in domestic cats.

Are cats girly? Of course they are. Living with a cat is like having Norah Jones singing just for you, in your living room. But a cat is more than just sensuous allure. It is a super-efficient hunter, an aggressive predator, and in my books predation is a guy thing. More than feminine or masculine, the cats I treat each day are family. We can't help it. Live with one and you come to know who it feels, how it thinks.

Yesterday morning a cat very personally reminded me of our compulsion to care, to nurture a fellow living thing, especially if you think of it as 'family'. A 19-year-old, longhaired black cat named Polly was brought in by a new client. Polly's eyes are grey, and her coat thinning, but she has the grace and dignity common to all older cats. I stroked her back, and she raised her butt, walked over and gave my leg a fully body rub, then she

jumped up onto my desk chair, curled up and stared at me. I told Polly's owner that my daughter Emily once had a cat, also named Polly, that had lived at my veterinary clinic after her first owner had died and who used to sit on my desk chair just like that before Emily took her in. Ten years ago, when Emily moved abroad, her best friend asked if she could have Polly. When I mentioned Emily's friend's name my new client explained that was who she got her Polly from eight years ago. The elderly cat sitting on my chair was the Polly I knew when she was in her prime and suddenly, it wasn't Norah Jones singing in my mind but Judy Collins lamenting "Who knows where the time goes". Over one third of our pet cats are classified as 'elderly' and that's why I've devoted the last part of this book to how to make life better for them. Polly needs a one hundred thousand mile service and some medicines but she has a wonderful and caring person looking after her, and by sheer serendipity a vet with more than a usual interest in ensuring her final years are filled with comfort and dignity.

20 essential tips for a new cat

1 You've acquired a cat, not a human in disguise. Be a good parent to your new cat, but it's not a furry child in disguise. Understand your cat's feline physical and mental needs. Respect your cat for what it is, a usually self-contained and intelligent individual who thinks like a cat, not like a lover or a child.

2 Understand feline body language, especially if you're a dog person and new to cats. Ear and tail activities, for example have dramatically different meanings.

3 Early and consistent contact with people during the first seven weeks of life is vital for a cat to be confident and friendly as an adult. Cats raised from birth inside people's homes are more likely to be sociable than those raised elsewhere.

4 Before you acquire a cat, decide whether or not you will let it outdoors. Assess the risks and if your cat is not allowed to go outdoors, train it to return home when it hears your voice.

5 Keep your cat carrier open, in a warm spot, and available for your cat to use at all times. This ensures that your cat will be more comfortable when you use the carrier for transport to the vet's.

6 Cats body language is much more subtle than that of dogs, or people. Become a careful observer. Even subtle changes in attitude or activity can be significant. If your cat is not behaving as it always does, contact your vet for advice.

7 Set aside at least ten minutes of each day for one-to-one special time with your cat. Use it for training or just for bonding.

8 Unless you are happy for your cat to treat you as unpaid staff, create rules and stick to them. And be consistent; cats are brilliant at finding inconsistencies and them working on them.

9 Cats love warmth. Ensure there's a warm spot, preferably in the sun, that your cat can always safely and securely retreat to.

10 Cats are visually orientated. Use moving objects to capture your cat's attention, for play or for training. Have sensible expectations during play. Your cat is a cat, not a cuddle machine.

11 When training your cat, good timing is essential. Earn your cat's respect through rewards, never through harshness. Fear and stress in cats inhibits their ability to concentrate and learn.

12 Clickers are great, but don't rely on them alone for training. If you are using a clicker as a "marker" get some professional help initially to learn the precision timing that is needed for this efficient method of training to be successful.

13 Good motivational training is based on good communication. After-the-fact discipline doesn't work. Your cat understands cause and immediate effect, not cause and delayed effect. Reprimand indirectly when you see unwanted behaviour such as scratching the furniture happening, not after you've found the damage.

14 When giving your cat a request, keep your tone of voice calm, not harsh or loud. Cats understand not so much what you say as how you say it.

15 Cats, unlike dogs, are usually sensible in their eating habits. Offer bones to your new cat. Chewing on bones is the best way to massage the gums and clean the teeth, both of which are necessary to prevent future tooth and gum disease.

16 Scratching visible objects is a natural and necessary cat activity. Don't amputate your cat's claws. Instead, provide a centrally located and attractive scratching post and train you cat to use that and not other objects.

17 Behaviour problems increase in direct proportion to how many cats you have. Expect behaviour concerns such as urine marking or furniture scratching to increase in multiple-cat households.

18 Cats don't broadcast when they are unwell, but joint pain is to be expected in older cats. Monitor jumping up and getting down; if your cat becomes tentative, have it checked by your vet. Painkillers are very efficient.

19 Watch your cat's weight and monitor its water consumption. Sugar diabetes is increasing in cats as fast as it is in people, so increased thirst always warrants a veterinary examination.

20 Never give dog (or human) medicines to your cat without first checking with your vet. Even seemingly safe treatments, or medicines such as spot-on flea control products for dogs or tablet painkillers for people, can kill cats with a single dose.

Chapter 1
Becoming a cat owner

The domesticated cat

We know the domestic cat emerged somewhere in the Fertile Crescent, the river-rich land that arcs from the Nile river in Egypt up through present day Israel, Lebanon, and Syria into southern Turkey, then folds back on itself and follows the Tigris and Euphrates rivers through Iraq and Iran down to the Persian Gulf. Here, around 10,000 years ago, some local wildcats actively chose to move into the first agricultural settlements our ancestors created. At least five different females from the wildcat population made this transition from savannah to village. All of today's more than 600 million domestic cats descend from these five matriarchs.

The cat walked in by itself

We didn't domesticate the cat. And when that local subspecies of wildcat, technically called *Felis silvestris lybica*, chose to live with us those thousands of years ago, it wasn't even the first wild animal that wanted to live in close proximity to people. The development of agriculture in the Fertile Crescent – the domestication and growth of wheat, barley, and rye – created a new and unique biological niche for other species too. Judging from the number of mouse skeletons found in the archaeological excavations of ancient dwellings, the aboriginal mouse was perhaps the first species to take advantage of this niche,

rapidly evolving into the "house mouse" we know today. Local wildcats were attracted to the concentration of rodents in agricultural settlements. They found that this new man-made ecological slot protected them from the larger predators in the region, but only those five females that were successful in controlling their fight-or-flight response when near to humans succeeded in moving into human settlements and multiplying there. It then took only a short time (relatively speaking) for natural selection to make this form of self-control – the ability to stay calm in the presence of humans – a prominent characteristic within the "tame wildcat" population. These cats

now lived in a symbiotic existence with people. They were tolerated primarily because they were useful, but also I'm sure because, especially as kittens, they were physically attractive too.

Wildcat relations

Throughout the world there is always a role for efficient small predators, and across Africa, Asia, and Europe there are in total five subspecies of wildcat that fill that niche. Although now surviving only in protected pockets of territory, the European wildcat (*F. silvestris silvestris*) once existed from Scotland down to the Iberian Peninsula and eastwards through Italy and the Balkans to Turkey and

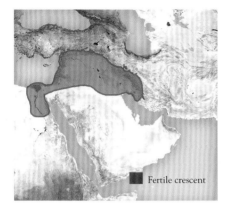

Fertile crescent

Above *It's a popular myth that the domestic cat emerged in Egypt. In fact, it may have evolved anywhere in the shaded area: the Fertile Crescent could be called the Feline Crescent.*

Right *Although the domestic cat is named as a subspecies of wildcat, it arose directly from just one of the five wild types, with no other genetic input.*

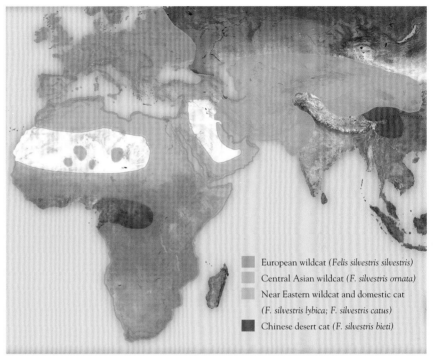

European wildcat (*Felis silvestris silvestris*)
Central Asian wildcat (*F. silvestris ornata*)
Near Eastern wildcat and domestic cat
(*F. silvestris lybica; F. silvestris catus*)
Chinese desert cat (*F. silvestris bieti*)

across to Georgia on the eastern shore of the Black Sea. This is not an ancestor of Europe's domestic cats.

The true ancestor, once called the African wildcat but now more accurately named the Near Eastern wildcat (*F. silvestris lybica*), existed throughout Mediterranean Africa from Morocco to Egypt, through the Arabian Peninsula to the Persian Gulf, and north to the Caspian Sea, where its territory merged with that of the Central Asian wildcat (*F. silvestris ornata*). This Asian subspecies exists from Iran, through Afghanistan and the other "stans" to China, where it meets the smallest population of wildcats, the Chinese desert cat (*F. silvestris bieti*). Modern DNA studies have shown that neither *F. silvestris ornata* nor *F. silvestris bieti* are ancestors of our housecats.

The fifth subspecies, the Southern African wildcat (*F. silvestris cafra*) lives in sub-Saharan Africa. This is a population of *F. silvestris lybica* that became isolated south of the Sahara so long ago that it evolved into a new genetic subspecies, which, unlike its parent, played no role in the evolution of *F. silvestris catus*, the domestic cat.

Early development
In the wild, female Near Eastern wildcats have been seen to care for the young of their sisters or mothers. This additional and unusual ability, to live in proximity to other wildcats, is another factor in the taming of the wildcat and its eventual evolution into the domestic cat.

Those individuals willing to share their new ecological niche within the

human settlement with other cats were most likely to breed and perpetuate this behaviour. Their kittens were the most likely to be hand-reared or fed by people. In time, those individuals that perpetuated dependent, kitten-like behaviour into adulthood were the most likely to survive and breed. The cat's behaviour was now being determined not only by natural selection, but also by human intervention.

These influences lead to physical and physiological modifications to these cats. Because it was no longer necessary to patrol an extensive terrain, regions of the brain needed for mapping a large territory became smaller. In fact, there was so much less for the brain to do that it shrank considerably, by almost 25 per cent. Similarly, because the fight-or-flight

This ticked and striped coat was worn by domestic cats in ancient Egypt, with solid colours and bi-colours emerging as cats spread across the Mediterranean.

THE DOMESTIC CAT'S CLOSEST RELATIVES

Researchers examining wildcat DNA found that 15 wildcats collected from the deserts of Israel, the United Arab Emirates, Bahrain, and Saudi Arabia were most closely related to the domestic cat.

response was no longer as vital for life, the adrenal and pituitary glands shrank. And because camouflage was no longer essential, cats with recessive coat colours survived and multiplied.

Yet for all these changes, most of us innately know that cats aren't really domesticated in the classic sense. They remain self-sufficient, and they still retain brilliant hunting skills, even when offered the most succulent food. Not just in form but also in function, our pet cats remain amazingly similar to their wild ancestors.

The voyage to Egypt

"Tamed" Near Eastern wildcats were taken out of the Fertile Crescent at least 9,000 years ago. At a human burial site from that date in Cyprus, French archeologists found the complete skeleton of an eight-month-old cat buried with its human owner, both skeletons aligned westward, towards the setting sun.

The island of Cyprus has no indigenous wildcats, so this cat or its ancestors must have been brought there by Neolithic people from what is now Turkey. They

Above *Not all of the mummified cats found in Egyptian cemeteries died naturally. Some offerings were perhaps prepared from excess kittens in temple grounds.*

Left *The domestic cat often appears beneath women's chairs in Egyptian art, representing fertility and motherhood, while dogs are shown with men.*

settled Cyprus, bringing with them their domesticated livestock, including cats. Over the following centuries, the tamed Near Eastern wildcat evolved both physically and behaviourally into the domesticated cat.

By 3,000 years ago, the powerful Egyptian civilization associated male cats with the sun god Ra and female cats with the fertility goddess Bast or Bastet. The cat attained such an important position in Egyptian religious life it became, in effect, deified. Unlike all other domesticated animals, the cat's outstanding value was to act as a "free agent", to come and go as it pleased. Keeping cats became common throughout Egypt. It was a way of showing respect for the gods, as well as controlling poisonous snakes and rodents.

Cats were tended both in life and in the afterlife, with great numbers preserved as mummies in special cat cemeteries. In the late 1800s, when British adventurers explored archeological sites in Egypt one firm exported back to Britain over 19 tons of cat mummies as fertilizer.

World travellers

The association with Egyptian deities, together with its natural vermin-killing abilities, increased the cat's value as a commodity and helped to ensure its expansion out of Egypt. The Egyptians prohibited the export of cats, but there is no doubt that Phoenician traders nonetheless transported domesticated felines throughout the Mediterranean. Subsequently, the Roman conquest of Egypt led to the cat spreading throughout the Roman Empire.

In large populations of random-bred cats, dominant genetic traits, such as tabby patterns and bi-colour coats, are most common.

In the Far East, cats fulfilled the same role of vermin and snake killers as in the Mediterranean but, just like dogs, they were also consumed during times of starvation. This unique role for the cat in southeast Asia evolved into today's culturally ambivalent attitude towards felines. While some are treasured as family companions and others are respected for their value as rodent hunters, millions are annually slaughtered and eaten in southern China, Korea, Vietnam, the Philippines and elsewhere. In Korea, dog consumption is dropping, but consumption of soup made from boiled cat, said to act as a tonic for elderly women, is increasing as the population of older women rises.

Mutations naturally occur

New lands brought new conditions, where new mutations flourished. The domestic cats that spread east from Egypt and the Fertile Crescent along trade routes to India and onwards to Burma and Siam found themselves in isolated pockets in the warmer Orient. There they evolved into the leaner, lighter-coloured breeds that came to be classified as the Orientals or "foreigns".

Other cats that accompanied traders and travellers east on the high-altitude silk routes to China became isolated in the cold mountains of Anatolia, the Caucasus and Persia – what are now the modern states of Turkey, the Russian Federation, and Iran – and there the mutation for long hair appeared, perhaps more than once. This remains a rugged region. One isolated population in the northeastern mountains of Turkey perpetuated their "founder" characteristic of orange-and-dominant-white, a feature of what is now called the Turkish Van.

The Van is a "natural" ancient breed, with a distinctive coat pattern developed in isolation.

TURKISH VAN	
Date of origin	Before 1700s
Place of origin	Turkey
Ancestry	Household cats
Weight range	3–8.5kg (7–19lb)
Colours	Traditional Western self and tortie colours in solid or tabby patterns, as van-pattern bi-colour only
Breed registries	GCCF FIFé CFA TICA

MANX	
Date of origin	Before 1700s
Place of origin	Isle of Man
Ancestry	Household cats
Weight range	3.5–5.5kg (8–12lb)
Colours	All self and tortie colours and bi-colours, in solid, smoke, and tipped, in Western tabby patterns and pointed pattern
Breed registries	GCCF FIFé CFA TICA

The unique Manx mutation can cause complete taillessness – and, unfortunately, health problems.

The founder effect

The characteristics and qualities of parents are passed on to their offspring in their genes. These characteristics can relate to health – for example, a predisposition to kidney diseases is passed on by around 40 per cent of Persian cat parents to their kittens. They can relate to personality – such as the increased and strident use of voice in the Siamese. And of course they can be associated with looks, the prime motive for selectively breeding "purebred" cats.

Genetic mutations are always occurring, but in large populations of cats breeding on their own, they usually vanish in a short length of time. In small, isolated populations (such as those first cats in the Lake Van region of Turkey) the long-term genetic influence of early members of the cat population is called the "founder effect" and has a powerful influence on resulting generations. The founder effect is why short tails were perpetuated only in isolated populations on the Isle of Man, Japan, and the Kuril Islands, or why extra toes (a trait known as polydactyly) are more common in free-breeding cats in and around Boston,

Massachusetts, and Halifax, Nova Scotia than anywhere else in the world.

Changing coat colours and patterns

With domestication, the cat's wild, tabby hunting camouflage was no longer essential for survival. Some experts have suggested that there is a relationship between "tameability" and the "solid" colours that emerged in domesticated cats, although there is as yet no genetic evidence to support this suggestion. I think these colours were perpetuated simply because we found them aesthetically appealing.

Technically speaking, there are two components to melanin, the natural substance that produces hair colour. One component, phaeomelanin, produces red or yellow while the other, eumelanin, produces black or brown. White hair contains no colour-producing melanin.

Wildcat hair has alternating bands of pale and dark pigment in a pattern called "agouti". All of the potential for different colours and body shapes existed before cats were transported out of the Fertile Crescent and around the world, but with domestication, different hair-colour variations increased in frequency.

The most dramatic of these was non-agouti hair, with only a single colour in it. Cats with single-coloured non-agouti coats are called solid or "self". Agouti is a dominant gene, so a cat needs to carry only one copy of this gene for the coat to be agouti. Non-agouti is a recessive gene, meaning a cat needs to carry two copies for it to be expressed in a solid colour. Either the founder effect in isolated populations or active human intervention

JAPANESE BOBTAIL	
Date of origin	before 1800s
Place of origin	Japan
Ancestry	Household cats
Weight range	2.5–4kg (6–9lb)
Colours	All self and tortie colours and bi-colours in solid and traditional tabby patterns
Breed registries	FIFé CFA TICA

The Jananese and Kurilian Bobtails carry the same genetic mutation for a short, curly tail.

COLOURS AND PATTERNS DEFINED

Agouti has several bands of colour in a single hair, and is the colour of the pale areas on tabby cats. The Abyssinian is agouti all over.

Tabby means dark markings (spots, swirls, or more commonly stripes) on a paler background. The stripe is solid colour, going right to the root, while the background colour is agouti. Tabby variations are:

- Classic or blotched, with dark stripes down the back and dark swirls on the sides of the body
- Mackerel or striped, with vertical unbroken lines on the flanks
- Spotted, with vertical lines broken into round spots
- Ticked, with just a little tabby striping in the legs

Solid or **self** has only one colour all over, with no agouti banding.

Dilute colours are paler, black becoming grey (called blue) and red becoming cream, and may be called "maltesed" or "caramelised".

Pointed means a pale body with dark legs, face, and tail, like a Siamese.

- Sepia or Burmese pointing has less contrast between a dark body and darker points
- Mink or Tonkinese pointing is part way between the two

Bi-colour is any colour and white, in any proportions from mitted to Van.

Tortoiseshell is the mixing of a eumelanistic and a phaeomelanistic colour, for example black and red, or blue and cream. Almost all tortie or tortie-and-white cats are female.

Brindle is tortoiseshell with intermingled colours.

Calico is tortoiseshell and white.

Mitted is bi-colour with just white booties on all feet.

Van is almost entirely white bi-colour, with a colour on the tail and between the ears.

Chinchilla or tipped is silver hair with coloured tips

Shaded is silver hair shafts with tip colour extending further down the hair shafts.

Smoke is silver hair with tip colour almost to the roots.

All cats, even solid colours, carry a gene for one of the tabby patterns.

Pointing can range from dramatic contrast to subtle shading, and appear in any coat type or base colour.

in larger populations ensured that non-agouti, solid colours emerged early in cat breeding.

Distinct cat populations

All of our 600 million domestic cats descend from five regional genetic groups: cats from western Europe, from the Mediterranean basin, from south-east Asia, from northern Asia, and from east Africa. Only one new breed, the Sokoke, is related to the east African genetic group, while North American, Australian and New Zealand random-bred cats are genetically identical to cats from Western Europe.

Some cat registries describe certain breeds as "natural", as regional varieties that pre-date human intervention in cat breeding; but vets at the University of California investigating the genetic make-up of many breeds made surprising discoveries. For example, the Japanese Bobtail is not genetically very Japanese: it was developed largely from European stock, which is why its colours are more "western" than "eastern". The Persian is also genetically European, now unrelated to the longhaired cats in Turkey, Iran (Persia), or southern Russia where it is said to have originated as a breed. Cat breed registries are complicated. Not all breeds are recognized by all the registries, or a breed might have one name in one register and a different name in another.

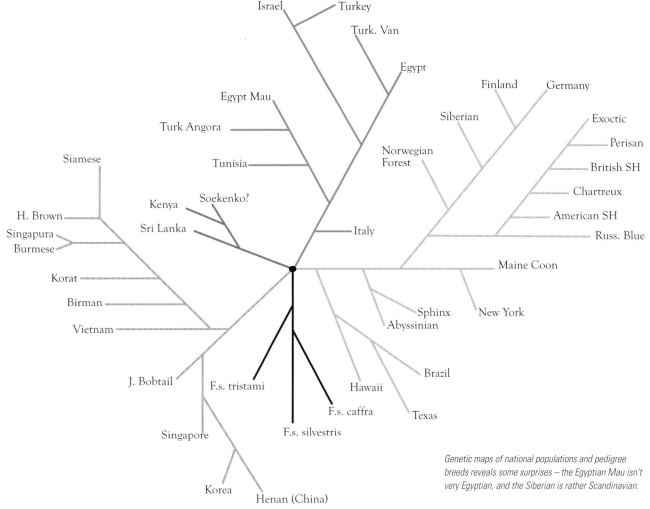

Israel   Turkey
Turk. Van
Egypt
Finland   Germany
Egypt Mau
Siberian   Exotic
Turk Angora   Perisan
Norwegian   British SH
Tunisia   Forest
Siamese   Chartreux
Kenya   Soekenko?   American SH
H. Brown   Sri Lanka   Russ. Blue
Singapura   Italy
Burmese   Maine Coon
Korat
Birman   Sphinx   New York
Vietnam   Abyssinian
J. Bobtail   F.s. tristami   Brazil
Hawaii
F.s. caffra   Texas
Singapore   F.s. silvestris
Korea
Henan (China)

Genetic maps of national populations and pedigree breeds reveals some surprises – the Egyptian Mau isn't very Egyptian, and the Siberian is rather Scandinavian.

Breed registries set rules and regulations concerning which breeds they will register. In parts of Europe, certain breeds are not recognized at all by the major registries because of what are – in my opinion, rightly – considered harmful deformities. These include the Manx and Cymric (because of spinal problems related to the tailless mutation), the Munchkin (because it's a skeletal dwarf), the Scottish Fold (because of skeletal problems), the Sphynx (because perpetuating hairlessness is considered detrimental to cats), and blue-eyed whites (because of associated deafness). In the United States, hybrids such as the Bengal, one of the most popular breeds in the

United Kingdom, are not recognized by the CFA, the largest breed registry.

The University of California genetic studies make defining a breed even more complicated. The Burmese and Singapura could not be told apart genetically by the standard used for most of the breeds, nor could the Siamese and Havana Brown. The Persian and Exotic Shorthair are unsurprisingly undifferentiated – but unexpectedly, so are the Birman and Korat. On the other hand, two breeds thought to be very closely related, the Turkish Angora and Turkish Van, aren't. In the dog world, different breeds evolved to do different things: to help in the hunt, to guard, to protect, to fight, to cuddle.

Most canine breeds are genetically very distinct from each other. In the cat world, one breed may differ from another by just a single gene affecting its hair.

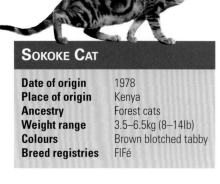

SOKOKE CAT

Date of origin	1978
Place of origin	Kenya
Ancestry	Forest cats
Weight range	3.5–6.5kg (8–14lb)
Colours	Brown blotched tabby
Breed registries	FIFé

Although quirky breeds are a growth area, traditional breed types are still widely popular. The wild-looking, longhaired Norwegian Forest Cat (right) and Maine Coon were more recently joined by the Siberian.

The future

Most "traditional" breeds were developed in Europe, primarily in Britain and France, within the last 150 years. But almost half of the 140 breeds recognized by one cat fancy or another, or under active development, have been created within the last 20 years – and most of them in North America. Certain trends are apparent and bound to continue.

Mix-and-match crossbreeding is good for cats. For example, crossing Siamese cats with other cats with solid or tabby colours to produce the Orientals increases genetic diversity in the resulting cats.

Hybridization, the crossing of the domestic cat with a non-domesticated wildcat, seems on the basis of the results with the Bengal to be neutral. It takes at least seven generations from the hybrid cross before the wildness of the wild cat is controlled (and I have one client who was hospitalized after an attack from her Bengal), but the Bengal experiment has now produced a healthy, attractive and generally amenable new breed. If the CFA were to recognize this breed, it could help control the high level of basement or backyard breeding that takes place, often with no thought to the well-being of the cats, their kittens, or their future owners.

Trademarking, as with the Ragdoll and related cats, is simply a business proposition. The breeds themselves are attractive in looks, personality, and health, which are more important.

Breeding for coat anomalies worries me a little. Curly or "rexed" coats have appeared and been selectively bred for in Britain (Cornish and Devon Rex),

The Bengal remains controversial globally, but as it moves further from the original hybrid cross it is becoming a breed with a viable long-term future.

Bengal	
Date of origin	1983
Place of origin	United States
Ancestry	Asian leopard cat, household cats, Egyptian Mau, Indian street cats
Weight range	5.5–10kg (12–22lb)
Colours	Brown marbled and spotted tabby and pointed tabby
Breed registries	GCCF FIFé TICA

America (American Rex, Selkirk Rex, LaPerm, and American Wirehair), and Germany (German Rex). While some rexed coats such as the Cornish Rex have insulating down, others don't, and it is not appropriate for these cats to venture outdoors in cold climates. The whiskers, an important part of a cat's sensory apparatus, may be brittle or absent on cats with curly hair mutations. Some curly longhair varieties are particularly prone to matting, as is the modern Persian's coat. Better to breed for long guard hair, as in the Maine Coon, Siberian, and Norwegian Forest Cats, than for long, wispy down.

Breeding for anatomical anomalies worries me a lot! The severe flat face of the show Persian is simply dreadful. With such a flat face, tears from the eyes can't drain into the nose so they overflow, causing skin inflammation. Nostrils are so tight that breathing can be difficult. The eyes are so prominent they can't be covered properly by tears and become inflamed. Teeth are displaced, and the cat can't groom itself properly. All of this on top of a wispy, downy coat that demands daily attention, otherwise it mats terribly. Having turned a masterpiece of form and function into such a disaster, we're now intentionally creating other breeds with anatomical mistakes: dwarfed cats such as the Munchkin, naked cats such as the Sphynx, genetically defective cats such as the Scottish Fold. No breed registry should accept as a new breed any form of cat that cannot do what all cats should be capable of doing: leading active, healthy

Curly haired cats may seem just like curly haired people, but rexing mutations can affect the nature of the coat in other ways.

lives, living long, and reproducing easily. Genetic engineering and cloning also worry me. One business already claims it has genetically engineered a hypoallergenic cat, although this is questioned. Korean scientists went a stage further: they cloned a cat but also genetically modified it by inserting a fluorescent gene so that the clones glowed in the dark.

Breeds with a reputation for reserve, like the British and European types, are losing ground to cuddly cats today – even though the image isn't fully deserved.

Cloning produces the equivalent of an identical twin, but it doesn't produce copycat personalities. Cats were first cloned early this century, and I'm glad to say there's been no major public interest in cloning pet cats.

CORNISH REX

Date of origin	1950s
Place of origin	Great Britain
Ancestry	Farm cat
Weight range	2.5–4.5kg (6–10lb)
Colours	All colours, shades, and patterns
Breed registries	GCCF FIFé CFA TICA

Domestic cat types and breeds

The earliest varieties of cats were lean, lithe, moderately sized, and fine coated, much like the Near Eastern wildcat from which they evolved. Short hair was, and still is, the most practical coat to wear in temperate and warm climates. Cats that moved out of the Mediterranean basin into western Europe developed more compact, stocky bodies, while those that spread into south-east Asia became lighter, with thinner, sparser coats of guard hair containing less insulating down, which helped them to radiate excess heat. These Eastern cats created a genetic cluster that is now referred to as the Oriental or foreign group of cats, complete with new colours.

Western and Eastern colours

Traditionally, "Western" cat coat colours are black, red, and their variations, while "Eastern" colours are chocolate and cinnamon and their variations, but this distinction is to some extent artificial. Black and red, together with their dilute versions blue (grey) and cream, and tabby patterns, are and always have been present in Eastern cats as well as Western ones. However, the mutations for chocolate and cinnamon did probably occur in the East. The mutation for dilute colours also probably arose in Asia, spreading back into Europe via Russia. These colours gave Asian cats distinctive hues as well as shapes that differentiated them from Mediterranean and western European cats.

Southeast Asian breeds

Genetically speaking, the south-east Asian breeds – the Siamese, Balinese, Burmese, Tonkinese, Singapura, Korat, and Birman – remain closely related to street cats in China, Vietnam, Korea, and Singapore today.

The Siamese pointed coat pattern originated somewhere in Asia at least 500 years ago, and has become most strongly associated with Thailand. These striking pointed cats attracted the attention of visitors, who brought them to the West in the 19th century.

Modern Siamese resemble catwalk models: the pattern is available even in moggies, without the extreme looks.

At first, both pointed and non-pointed solid-coloured cats from the East were called Siamese, but by the 1920s only pointed cats with blue eyes could use the name. Non-pointed cats eventually became today's Orientals, known for a time as Foreigns in the United Kingdom. Siamese cats also occasionally produced

SIAMESE	
Date of origin	Pre-1700s
Place of origin	Thailand (formerly Siam)
Ancestry	Household and temple cats
Weight range	2.5–5.5kg (6–12lb)
Colours	All solid self and tortie colours and tabbies, with Siamese pointed pattern
Breed registries	GCCF FIFé CFA TICA TCA

The eyes of Orientals can be influenced by the Siamese pointing they carry beneath their coat colour, giving a range of alluring blue-tinted green shades alongside clear greens and golds.

CONFUSING NAMES

The name Havana has two different meanings. In Britain, a solid chocolate of Siamese type was developed in the 1950s, and while the colour was called Havana, the breed was registered as Chestnut Brown Foreign. That colour eventually became part of the Oriental Shorthair. Havanas were exported to the United States, where they became the foundation of a separate breed, the Havana Brown. This remains very rare.

pointed longhaired kittens, and those have been developed into the Balinese. Geneticists have confirmed that the American breed called the Havana Brown is simply a solid-coloured Siamese.

Siamese adult coat colour is different from kitten coat colour. Kittens and young cats have paler points or markings, while older cats have darker body colour. The air temperature also affects point colour. Pointed cats that go outdoors in cold climates have darker ears, legs, and tails than those that live in warmer climates. A fever or even bandaging a leg can reduce the intensity of darker point colour. Even shaving the belly for a neutering operating can lead to new hair growing back in the area slightly lighter in colour.

There were solid and tabby cats among the first cats brought to the West from Siam (now Thailand), but when the Siamese Club of Great Britain declared that the name Siamese should apply to only blue-eyed, pointed cats, the other coat colours fell into decline. Eventually, recognition of the Chestnut Brown Foreign as a separate breed in the United Kingdom led to the development of the group. The Chestnut eventually became the Havana, classed first as a Foreign and now as a colour of the Oriental breed; it is separate from the breed called the Havana Brown in the United States. The coat is very short and fine, with a glossy sheen, and needs little attention, but it also provides little

Orientals, which come in Shorthair and Longhair versions, are Siamese in a solid or tabby wrapper.

ORIENTAL SHORTHAIR

Date of origin	1950s
Place of origin	Great Britain
Ancestry	Siamese, Korat, Shorthairs
Weight range	4–6.5kg (9-14lb)
Colours	All colours, patterns, and shades except pointed sepia, and mink; many colours have special names
Breed registries	GCCF FIFé CFA TICA

THAILAND'S BOOK OF CAT POEMS

While only black cats are associated with luck in the west (good in Europe, bad in America), in Thailand all kinds of cats were more frequently associated with good luck than with bad omens. The *Tamra Maew* or *Cat Book Poems*, in Thailand's National Library in Bangkok, contains illustrations of seventeen good-luck cats, including cats that are strikingly similar to today's Siamese, Burmese, and Korat, and six bad luck cats, including cats that eat their kittens, cats with kinked tails, white cats with red-brown eyes, and tiger-striped tabbies. The illustrations are the best evidence of the varieties of cats inhabiting what was then Siam in the 14th century.

BALINESE	
Date of origin	1950s
Place of origin	United States
Ancestry	Longhaired Siamese
Weight range	2.5–5kg (6–11lb)
Colours	All self and tortie colours and tabby patterns, in pointed pattern
Breed registries	GCCF FIFé CFA TICA TCA

Above *A single gene makes the difference between the shorthaired Siamese (and Colorpoint Shorthair in CFA) and the longhaired Balinese (and Javanese in CFA).*

Below *The Burmese or sepia pointing pattern is more obvious on lighter colours than in the original sable. American cats have rounder faces than European ones.*

insulation in cold weather. Lean and lithe in build, they have large ears on a long, triangular head and a svelte body carried on long, slim legs, but despite this delicate appearance, these are long-lived cats with a median life expectancy of over 17 years. The typical Oriental character matches these looks, being active, playful, athletic, and notoriously gregarious.

A longhaired Siamese was registered in Britain as long ago as 1928, and as a recessive trait it is certainly not improbable that this gene was carried by the very first Siamese brought to the West. These "sports" were usually sold as pets, but eventually recognized in American registries, and a decade later

Left *Orientals are bred in all tabby patterns: curiously the eastern-looking ticked was the last to be recognized in the United Kingdom.*

European ones. Following objections by Siamese breeders to the term longhaired Siamese, they were named Balinese. The medium-long coat lies sleekly against the body, and its silky texture makes it relatively easy to care for. Like the Siamese, this is a highly inquisitive breed that will investigate corners of your home you never knew existed.

A slightly confusing situation exists with regard to the colours of these breeds. In Europe, a wide range of colours and even tabby patterns are allowed. In North America, the CFA and TCA recognize only the four "original" colours of seal, blue, chocolate, and lilac, just as in

the Siamese. Other colours and tabby points are classed as separate breeds, the Colorpoint Shorthair and Javanese.

Another south-east Asian export, the Burmese is defined mainly by the subtly shaded pattern of its fine satin-like coat, known as sepia. Although sepia-pointed cats were widely known in their homeland, the origins of all

BURMESE	
Date of origin	1930s
Place of origin	Myanmar (formerly Burma)
Ancestry	Temple cats, Siamese crosses, household cat crosses
Weight range	3.5–6.5kg (8–14lb)
Colours	All self colours with Burmese pointed pattern
Breed registries	GCCF FIFé CFA TICA TCA

SINGAPURA

Date of origin	1975
Place of origin	Singapore and United States
Ancestry	Burmese
Weight range	2-4 kg (4-9lb)
Colours	Sepia agouti
Breed registries	GCCF CFA TICA

The Singapura is an aesthetic recreation of Singapore's diminutive ferals rather than a genuine descendant, but none the less attractive for that.

Burmese cats can be traced back to a single cat, Wong Mau, a female brought from Burma (now Myanmar) to America in 1930. (Ironically, Wong Mau herself was genetically not a Burmese but in fact what is now called a Tonkinese, with one Siamese-pointing gene and one sepia.) The muscular body is surprisingly heavy, and I agree with the description that they feel like "bricks wrapped in silk". For many years the American Burmese came in any colour you liked, so long as it was sable (genetically black), but when American cats were imported into Britain the breed diverged to take two forms. European breeders prefer a more typically angular Oriental look and

The subtly patterned Tonkinese is a breed that can never breed completely true, producing variable offspring in every generation.

recognized a wider range of colours. Cats in South Africa, Australia, and New Zealand follow the European type. The European Burmese's head, the area which most differs from the American type, is a short wedge with a blunt muzzle, with widely-placed, rounded, and only slightly slanted eyes. Although it has a quieter and more relaxed personality than most other Oriental breeds, the Burmese still craves company, and some owners call them "Velcro cats" because of their propensity to cling. A medical curiosity is a condition called oro-

facial pain syndrome, which occurs only in some individual Burmese and breeds developed from it.

The Singapura has a ticked tabby coat, like the Abyssinian, overlaid with the sepia pointing pattern of the Burmese – from which it can scarcely be differentiated genetically. It is, in fact, a colour variation of the Burmese although some breeders still argue that it descends from feral "drain" cats in Singapore.

Pointed hybrids have existed probably for as long as the two pointing mutations that produced the Siamese and Burmese have existed, and the Tonkinese is simply a crossing of these two breeds, just like the founder of the Burmese breed. It was not until the 1950s, however, that breeders began to work on creating and refining crosses. Because the characteristic coat, called mink, is a

The Korat's sweet, heart-shaped face belies its strong personality.

TONKINESE

Date of origin	1960s
Place of origin	United States and Canada
Ancestry	Burmese and Siamese
Weight range	2.5–5.5kg (6–12lb)
Colours	All self and tortie colours except fawn and cinnamon, in solid and all tabby patterns, in mink pattern
Breed registries	GCCF CFA TICA

KORAT

Date of origin	Before 1700
Place of origin	Thailand
Ancestry	Asian household cats
Weight range	2.5–4.5kg (6–10lb)
Colours	Solid blue self
Breed registries	GCCF FIFé CFA TICA

BIRMAN

Date of origin	Unknown, recognized 1925
Place of origin	Myanmar (formerly Burma) and France
Ancestry	Asian household cats
Weight range	4.5–8kg (10–18lb)
Colours	All self and tortie colours and tabbies, in pointed pattern with white mittens
Breed registries	GCCF FIFé CFA TICA

Often suspected to be just an early pointed Persian crossbreed with a romantic tale attached, the Birman turns out to be genetically true to its name.

The Birman's blue eyes and golden body colour are said to have appeared in a miraculous transformation of a temple cat that inspired monks to defeat their attackers.

blend of two genetic patterns, all Tonks carry genes for both Siamese and Burmese pointing, and every mating may produce kittens of those patterns. Like all the true Asian breeds, Tonks have a greater-than-cat-average life expectancy.

The descriptive verses in Thailand's *Tamra Maew* or *Cat Book Poems* (1350–1767) distinguish the frosted silver Si-Sawat from other blue cats. Today this is called the Korat, a name taken from the province of Thailand that is its homeland. In the West the breed remains rare but fairly stable in numbers. The coat is short and fine, with no undercoat, and tipped with silver, an effect called "sea foam". A small number of individuals suffer from a recessive genetic neuromuscular disorder called gangliosidosis, and a screening programme is in place to eliminate this.

The Birman is close to the feline populations of both Vietnam and Burma (now Myanmar), and tradition has it that this breed is descended from a pair of shorthaired temple cats shipped to France in 1919 by the Khmer people as a gift of thanks for saving temples during Brahmin uprisings. Breeders in France added

the longhair gene but not much else; geneticists have to look in close detail to differentiate this breed from the Korat. The silky coat is not as thick and prone to matting as many other longhaired cats.

The GCCF's Asians aren't really Asian, but as they were developed from the Burmese (amongst others), and are the consequence of a breeding programme by one of my clients, the late Miranda von Kirchberg, I've included them here. From the original accidental mating of a Chinchilla longhair and a Burmese, creating the Burmilla, Miranda went on to create a whole new category of varying shaded hues, even a longhaired variety.

The Tiffanie (not to be confused with the Tiffany/Chantilly) is the longhaired member of the Asian group in the United Kingdom.

THE ASIAN GROUP

Date of origin	1981
Place of origin	Great Britain
Ancestry	Burmese, Chinchillas, non-pedigrees
Weight range	4–7kg (9–15lb)
Colours	Traditional Western and Eastern self and tortie colours in solid, smoke, and shaded, and tabby and sepia patterns; some colours have special names
Breed registries	GCCF FIFé (some)

Solid-coloured cats

Non-agouti, solid-coloured coats have existed almost from the time cats entered into our protection and are ubiquitous throughout the feline world. The grey colour, called blue by breeders, was particularly coveted in Europe because it was rare: it probably originated in Asia then spread from there into Russia and on to Europe. Breeders created several breeds in this and other recessive solid colours that breed true.

However they arrived, via Russia or (as legend has it) with crusaders returning from the Middle East, by the 18th century, solid grey cats called Chartreux were so well established that they were described by the naturalist Buffon as "the cat of France". The dense, velvety blue coat was also much prized by furriers. Colonies existed throughout France, but by the end of World War II the breed was almost extinct. Breeders preserved the cat by crossing survivors with British Blue Shorthairs. This is why its body is stocky, like British Shorthairs.

The Russian Blue has been accepted as a breed since the 19th century and was at one time called the Archangel Cat, after the northern Russian port. It declined in the early 20th century but was revived in the 1950s. More recently, using cats from Russia, breeders have developed solid black (Russian Black) and solid white (Russian White) varieties; some registries now classify all Russian solid-coloured cats as Russian Shorthairs. Like the Chartreux, the Russian Blue is muscular, but it is large and somewhat leaner looking, with limpid green eyes.

In it's homeland, the Russian Blue is considered a lucky gift.

Romantically named for a Carthusian monastery, the Chartreux has been the favoured pet of French notables from President de Gaulle to the author Collette.

CHARTREUX

Date of origin	Before 1700s
Place of origin	France
Ancestry	Household cats
Weight range	3–7.5kg (7–17lb)
Colours	Blue self only
Breed registries	FIFé CFA TICA

RUSSIAN BLUE AND RUSSIAN SHORTHAIRS

Date of origin	Before 1800s
Place of origin	Russia
Ancestry	Household cats
Weight range	3–5.5kg (7–12lb)
Colours	Blue, black, white
Breed registries	GCCF FIFé CFA TICA

THE BRITISH BLUE

The big, muscular cat once known as the British Blue is an extremely popular cat in Britain, although, because all colour varieties are recognized the expanded breed is called the British Shorthair (*see* page 36). The dense coat was created through crossbreeding with Persian cats and covers a heavily muscled body. When I take a blood sample from a British Blue's foreleg I have something with substance I can hold on to! Its chubby cheeks and sleek coat led to it being used in a cat food commercial (hard-working professional woman comes home to an adoring and sensuous British Blue) that was so successful the manufacturers could not meet the demand for the food.

When blue cats from Russia were first shown in France and Britain, both shorthaired and longhaired types were seen. The shorthairs went on to become the Russian Blue but the longhairs were largely forgotten. In the 1980s, the longhaired Russian Blue was recreated in the United States and curiously named Nebelung, after the German for mist.

The solid black Bombay is another American breed, created by using black American Shorthairs for their colour and sable Burmese for their build. The result is a muscular, glossy black cat with copper eyes. As often happens in catdom, in the United Kingdom the name Bombay refers to something completely different, the black Asian Shorthair. A similar situation exists with two other solid-coloured cats, the Havana Brown and Havana (*see* page 23).

BOMBAY

Date of origin	1960s
Place of origin	United States
Ancestry	American Shorthairs and Sable Burmese
Weight range	2.5–5kg (6–11lb)
Colours	Black
Breed registries	CFA TICA

NEBELUNG

Date of origin	1984
Place of origin	United States
Ancestry	Russian Blue, household cat
Weight range	2.5–5kg (6–11lb)
Colours	Blue
Breed registries	TICA TCA

A rare breed, the Nebelung emerged largely through the work of a single breeder.

Tabby pattern cats

In tabby patterns the darker hair is solid going right to the root while the background lighter colour is banded coloured agouti (*see* page 18). All the tabby patterns – stripes, swirls, spots, or simple ticking – are separate mutations of the tabby gene. The ticked or Abyssinian pattern is dominant over all; spots are dominant over the striped or mackerel pattern, which is dominant over the blotched or classic pattern. Because tabby was the original coat for domestic cats, breeders generally disregarded it until recently, when renewed interest in creating cat breeds that look "natural" has lead to several new tabby breeds.

Tabbys are everywhere
The tabby cat is ubiquitous around the world. There is classic, with dark stripes down the back and dark swirls on the sides of the body; mackerel with vertical unbroken lines; spotted with vertical lines broken into round spots, and ticked, with just a little tabby striping. The pattern is so common some people actually call all cats tabbies. I've lived with a classic tabby moggie (what registries call a "domestic shorthair") and a silver tabby Maine Coon with a perfect 'M' on her head. Garfield, the world's laziest cartoon cat, is of course a marmalade-coloured tabby tom. Virtually all of the regional shorthair and longhair breeds come in all varieties and colours including tabby patterns, but some breeds are restricted to these patterns. Because tabbies can carry hidden recessive solid-coloured genes, the odd non-tabby kitten will always appear.

Abyssinian and Somali
The dominant ticked tabby pattern is carried by the domestic cat's ancestor, the Near Eastern wildcat, and is a perfect camouflage, especially in the desert

Above: The Egyptian Mau was the first of the spotty tabby breeds, followed by the Ocicat in the 1960s.

Aby litters always produced the odd "fuzzy' kitten: in the 1960s, American and Canadian breeders decided to breed them rather than selling them as pets.

The Aby first appeared in Europe in the 19th century, with a cat brought back by troops from Abyssinia (now Ethiopa) winning a prize in London in 1871.

environment of the Middle East and North Africa. It has been present in the domestic cat from the start, but the only old breeds that are ticked tabbies are the Abyssinian and its longhaired version, the Somali.

This is one of my favourite breeds, not for its personality – they can be demanding and pushy – but for its looks. Always in the top ten registered cat breeds in North America, they have never gained quite the same level of popularity in Europe. The original colours were usual or ruddy (which is a black tabby), sorrel or red (which is cinnamon), and their dilutes, and the more conservative registries still accept only those colours. The ticked tabby pattern that characterizes this breed is controlled by a single gene and gives each hair alternating light and dark bands that result in a shimmering effect as the cat moves. There is a strong similarity between the Abyssinian and ancient Egyptian images. This breed can suffer from inherited forms of retinal atrophy, an eye problem seen more often in dogs.

ABYSSINIAN AND SOMALI

Date of origin	1860s
Place of origin	Ethiopia
Ancestry	Household and street cats
Weight range	4–7.5kg (9–17lb)
Colours	Traditional Western and Eastern colours in solid and shaded, in ticked tabby pattern
Breed registries	GCCF FIFé CFA TICA

The Ocicat is a happy accident, the unexpected offspring of a cross aimed at producing Siamese with ticked tabby points.

Ocicat

Although its name seems to imply that it belongs among the wild-cat hybrids, the Ocicat is the result of selectively breeding Abyssinians with Siamese and tabby American Shorthairs. The spotted tabby pattern of the Ocicat differs from that of most other breeds in that its spots are larger, round, and do not follow the lines of a mackerel or striped tabby. The coat is short and fine, and clothes a powerful athletic build with muscular legs. The breed shows its Siamese ancestry in its personality, being playful, talkative, and responding well to training when young. Because of the genes carried by its parent breeds, the Ocicat produces variants

in ticked and classic tabby patterns, as well as its own distinctive spotted coat. The Jungala was developed from these variants, and is essentially an Ocicat without the spots.

Egyptian Mau

Mau is the Egyptian word for cat, and tradition says this breed descends from Egyptian street cats. In fact it is genetically closer to the Turkish Angora and Tunisian street cats than to present day Egyptian cats (*see page 19*). The Mau does look very similar to cats depicted on Egyptian walls and scrolls, with a long, athletic body and spots that follow no discernable pattern. The eyes of the Mau differ from the ancient images, which show narrow, wild-looking eyes; those of the Mau are wide and rounded.

Hybridized cats

Many species in the cat family will produce offspring when crossed, and there have been big-cat hybrids in circuses and zoos over the years as a result of accidental or deliberate matings. In most cases, however,

While the Mau is intended to resemble the earliest Egyptian cats, some later mutations, like the shimmering smoke, were just too good to breed out.

OCICAT	
Date of origin	1964
Place of origin	United States
Ancestry	Siamese, Abyssinian, American Shorthairs
Weight range	2.5–6.5kg (6–14lb)
Colours	Brown, cinnamon, blue, or fawn solid and silver spotted tabbies
Breed registries	GCCF FIFé CFA TICA

EGYPTIAN MAU	
Date of origin	1950s
Place of origin	Egypt, Italy
Ancestry	Egyptian street cats, Italian household cats
Weight range	2.5–5kg (6-11lb)
Colours	Black in solid and silver in spotted tabby pattern only, and in smoke without tabby pattern but with strong "ghost" markings
Breed registries	GCCF FIFé CFA TICA

either the male or the female offspring are partially or completely infertile, making further development of the hybrid line difficult. The domestic cat can not only successfully mate with its closest wildcat relatives, it can also produce fertile female kittens when it is mated with more distant relatives such as the Asian leopard cat (*Prionailurus bengalensis*), the jungle cat (*Felis chaus*), and the African serval (*Leptailuris serval*). Wild-cat hybrids remain controversial. Male kittens of jungle cat and African serval crosses with domestic cats are infertile, and first generation pregnancies often abort because of the longer durations of pregnancies in the wildcats. Hybridization of the Asian leopard cat and domestic cat, producing the Bengal has, however, been successful, with over 100,000 descendants. It is now the third most registered breed in Britain, although in its homeland the CFA will not recognize it due to its hybrid origins.

Toyger

The quirkily named Toyger was produced by mixing and matching Bengals with mackerel tabby cats to create a tiger in miniature. It has been exported from the United States to Britain and Australia, and seems to have a good chance of wider acceptance. Every part of the Toyger is described as "muscular" in the breed standard. The short, thick coat has a sheen of "glitter" like that of the Bengal, and the striking striped pattern lacks the curved lines and dorsal stripe of a mackerel tabby.

WHAT GIVES A CAT ITS SPOTS?

The leopard may not be able to change its spots, but breeders certainly believe their cats are able to. The spots on cats often follow the vertical lines of the mackerel tabby, leading to a theory that the spotted tabby is simply a genetically dominant modification that "breaks" the lines. The coats of the Egyptian Mau and the Ocicat lack such a pattern, but these breeds produce variant kittens showing the classic tabby pattern, and their spotting might be a broken classic pattern instead. Another school of thought holds that there is at least one dominant gene that produces a spotted tabby pattern independently of any other pattern. There may be more to the spotted tabby than broken lines, but if the pattern is due to the subtle influences of many genes, it will be hard to determine.

CALIFORNIA SPANGLED AND AUSTRALIAN MIST

The lithe California Spangled, developed from Abyssinians, Siamese, and non-pedigree cats, was launched by an anti-fur breeder in 1986 in a catalogue (which ironically also contained fur coats). Recognized by TICA, it never gained popularity. It was bred in Western colours in solid, smoke, and silver in tabby pattern.

The people-orientated Australian Mist, Australia's first "homegrown" breed and still rare outside Australia, was developed from Abyssinians, Burmese and other non-pedigree cats. It comes in traditional eastern colours in spotted tabby.

Every tabby pattern is variable: just look at random-bred moggies to see the range of possibilities. In the Toyger, the aim is to mimic the flame-like stripes of a tiger.

Shorthairs

Recognized breeds of what are, in essence, excellent examples of regional cat populations have been developed, first in the United Kingdom and United States, then elsewhere in Europe, in South America and in Australasia. Their common characteristics are that they are usually accepted in every colour variation that cats are capable of appearing in, and usually shorthairs.

Population genetics

Before DNA studies were possible, population geneticists carried out brilliant work worldwide on cat coat colours. By investigating colours and understanding ancient trade routes, they were able to show that the non-agouti (usually solid black) mutation probably developed in either Greece or Lebanon (Phoenicia) around 2,500 years ago. Today it is found most frequently in northwest African cities, such as Tangiers and Rabat, and British port cities, such as Liverpool and Glasgow. Blotched tabby, although it probably originated in northeast Iran, increased along trade routes, reaching its

Originally regarded as a breed in itself, the British Blue was the first of the British Shorthairs, and remains the most popular colour.

highest concentration in Britain. From there it was disseminated throughout the British Empire, to North America from 1650 onwards and to Australia and New Zealand starting 100 years later. Our trading and transporting of cats had a consequential influence on the colours and patterns that predominated in the shorthair cat populations in countries or whole regions. One common denominator, however, is that in urban areas, non-agouti cats make up more than 50 per cent of the cat population. In shorthair breeds, it seems that non-agouti colours have been popular for centuries.

British Shorthair

The original founding stock for this breed was drawn from the sturdy everyday cats of Britain, and when the showing

CAT SHOWS

If you plan to visit a cat show, or are thinking of exhibiting your cat at one, expect the unexpected. Rules at cat shows can sometimes be positively Byzantine. For example, in North America the Cat Fanciers' Association (CFA) does not permit the showing of declawed cats, but The International Cat Association (TICA) does. In the UK, the Governing Council of the Cat Fancy (GCCF) permits cats to be shown at shows affiliated with the Federation International Feline (FIFé) but only if they are first informed and not within 13 days before or after a GCCF show.

BRITISH SHORTHAIR	
Date of origin	1880s
Place of origin	Britain
Ancestry	Household, street, and farm cats
Weight range	4–8kg (9–18lb)
Colours	All self and tortie colours and bi-colours, in solid, smoke, and tipped, in Western tabby patterns and pointed pattern
Breed registries	GCCF FIFé CFA TICA

and breeding of cats became popular in the late 19th century, this was the most popular breed in the very first British cat shows. The founder of the Cat Fancy in Britain, Harrison Weir, bred British Blues. The breed lost favour in the early part of the 20th century, and had almost died out by 1950. A concerted effort by breeders

The American Shorthair was originally called the Domestic Shorthair to reflect its everyday origins, but that is the name now given to random-bred cats when they are entered in shows.

Pedigrees guarantee consistency, but seen in isolation, some pedigree individuals look little different from the best of their random-bred compatriots.

revived its fortunes, and today the British Shorthair is once more the most popular pedigree cat in its native country. One curious trait that sets British Shorthairs apart is that almost half of all cats in the breed have Type B blood, a rare trait in the cat population at large.

BRAZIL'S NATIONAL BREED

The Brazilian Shorthair is an attempt to create an indigenous breed from Brazil's population of random-bred domestic cats. A breed standard was written for a strong, medium-sized cat with a short coat. The standard differs from British and European Shorthairs in a lighter build, longer head, and close-lying coat, suited to a warmer climate. The breed is rare, more common in the United States than in Brazil.

The word most used to describe the British Shorthair is cobby, which essentially means compact and solid. An unneutered male British Shorthair looks like a street brawler with a strong, muscular body, carried low on strong legs. Its broad, full face has a short, straight nose. The crisp coat is dense, weatherproof, and practical, although it requires a little help from time to time to keep it looking its best. The classic blues, tortoiseshells, and tabbies are still popular today, but the crosses made to revive the breed brought in new genes, and today a wide range of exotic colours and patterns is recognized in the breed in its home country, reflecting the increased diversity of the domestic cat population in general.

American Shorthair
Domestic cats arrived in North America with the first settlers, as early as the 1500s, and have been present in substantial numbers as working household

AMERICAN SHORTHAIR

Date of origin	1900s
Place of origin	United States
Ancestry	Domestic cats
Weight range	3.5–7kg (8–15lb)
Colours	Traditional Western self and tortie colours and bi-colours, in solid, smoke, shaded, or tipped, and classic or mackerel tabby
Breed registries	CFA TICA TCA

and farm animals since the 1700s. The pressures of the North American environment, with a wider range of natural predators than in Europe, ensured that these cats evolved into larger animals than their Old World counterparts, with powerful bodies on well-muscled legs. The short coat is thick and hard in texture to provide protection from cold, wet, and minor injuries. By the end of

The European Shorthair is a fine cat, but has not proved as much of a success as national breeds like the British Shorthair and the Chartreux.

long-lived, helped by an exemplary breed standard that disqualifies "any feature so exaggerated as to foster weakness".

European Shorthair

While there have been shorthaired cats in mainland Europe for over two millenia, the selectively bred "everyday" cats were initially classified within the British Shorthair. In 1982 FIFé created a new category for this breed, which started with an established type and a large breeding stock of cats from documented backgrounds. The breed's appearance is moderate in all respects. It has a medium to large, well-muscled body, but is not as heavily built or cobby as the British Shorthair, and the broad head is triangular to rounded, with large, round eyes and medium-sized, upright ears. The coat is short but dense, springy, and insulating, completing the picture of a sturdy, all-weather, all-purpose cat. The nature of the breed is also typically that of a European household cat, but permitted colours are not as extensive as they are for British Shorthairs.

Antipodean

This "everycat" breed was at first known as the New Zealand Shorthair: the name change reflects both the inclusion of a longhair standard and the increased work on the breed in Australia. Like other national breeds, it is drawn from typical household and working cats, descended from the cats that travelled with early settlers, mostly from Britain.

It is recognized only by New Zealand's indigenous cat registry. The Antipodean is medium-sized, of muscular build, and with a gently rounded, wedge-shaped head. There is a small subset of the breed, known as the Clippercat, which is essentially an Antipodean with extra toes. I understand how having a cat breed created from local random-bred cats enhances nationalism and pride in the country, but wonder what value there is in this form of selective breeding for "catdom" – that is, for the gene pool of the regional cats.

EUROPEAN SHORTHAIR	
Date of origin	1982
Place of origin	European mainland
Ancestry	Household cats, British Shorthair
Weight range	3.5–7kg (8–15lb)
Colours	Traditional Western self and tortie colours and bi-colours, in solid, smoke, and Western tabby patterns
Breed registries	FIFé

the 19th century, American breeders realized that the characteristics of their domestic cats were worth preserving. The Domestic Shorthair, as it was at first called, was the result. It was renamed the American Shorthair in 1966, and is popular in Canada and the United States but uncommon elsewhere. The American Shorthair is still bred to be robust and

ANTIPODEAN	
Date of origin	1990s
Place of origin	New Zealand and Australia
Ancestry	Household cats
Weight range	3.5–7kg (8–15lb)
Colours	Traditional Western self and tortie colours and bi-colours in solid, smoke, shaded, tipped, and tabby patterns
Breed registries	CATZ Inc

The cats that were the basis of Antipodean populations and the new breed are still similar to their European cousins, although with higher numbers of polydactyls.

Longhaired cats

The most popular coat length in all purebred cats in North America, the longhaired cat breeds range from the most genetically diverse, such as the Siberian, to genetic train wrecks, such as the show-quality, flat-faced Persian. Some longhair coats, such as the Maine Coon's, need only a little more daily grooming than thick, short coats, which I'm sure is one reason why this and other similar longhaired breeds are so rightly popular.

Rooted in the cat population

Longhaired cats spread into Europe hundreds of years ago and have been status-symbol pets ever since they arrived there. Official breed histories state that they were brought from Persia into Italy by Pietro della Valle and from Turkey into France by Nicolas-Claude Fabri de Pieresc, both in the early 17th century, but genetic evidence indicates that longhaired cats were imported directly into Scandinavia by the Vikings long before that. Those first longhair cats' coats were probably similar to that of the modern Turkish Angora, what is now called "semi-long", and this is perhaps closest to the original mutation. However or whenever the longhair trait really arrived, it eventually escaped the populations of prized imports and embedded itself in the local random-bred cat populations.

Because the long hair trait is genetically recessive, only a minority of random-bred cats have luxurious semi-long or long coats. This relative rarity in the random-bred population may be the

Although the official "Peke-faced" Persian is gone, mainstream Persians, especially in North America, now look almost as extreme.

reason why historically the most popular pedigree breeds tended to be longhaired. Even so, because purebreds are a tiny minority of all cats, the population of random-bred longhair cats in the world far exceeds the population of all longhaired pedigree breeds of cat.

Random-bred longhaired cats survived in colder climates, for example in Scandinavia and Russia, to form the basis for the Norwegian Forest Cat and the Siberian. They crossed the Atlantic to North America, where the longest, thickest coats naturally conveyed the greatest advantage in the cold continental winters. These natural survivors were the ancestors of the Maine Coon. The thick coat of these northern breeds is the result of the survival of the

CAT of ANGORA

It may not capture feline grace, but this 18th century illustration shows the longer ruff and britches characteristic of a semi-longhaired Angora.

The longhaired coat is determined by a single gene (called fibroblast growth factor 5). If a cat inherits inactive copies of this gene it will have a long coat. It's as simple as that. Other genes are responsible for the density, thickness or extraordinary length of some long coats. To reduce the grooming burden, or to overcome excessive matting, some longhaired cat owners, including those in my family, have their cats clipped short. If you do, don't be surprised if your usually placid cats becomes markedly more active and involved in family life. Many cats seem to enjoy freedom from their warm, heavy overcoats.

fittest. The Persian's luxurious coat, on the other hand, is the result of many generations of highly successful selective breeding for a prestige pet.

The Chinchilla is a tipped Persian, a sprinkle of black making the white coat sparkle, but also has a unique eye blue-green colour.

Persian

The Persian was one of the first breeds recognized in Britain, and by 1900 it was accepted in all existing registries in the world. Throughout the 20th century it was the most popular cat breed worldwide. It still is in North America, although in Britain breeds with longer life expectancies, the British Shorthair, Siamese, Ragdoll, Maine Coon, and Bengal, have overtaken it in only a decade.

The Persian has a sturdy-looking, cobby body with short, thick legs and a broad chest. The head is round, and the ears small, with plentiful tufts of fur at the base. The noses of early Persians were less compressed than those seen in today's

PERSIAN	
Date of origin	1800s
Place of origin	Great Britain
Ancestry	Longhaired Middle-Eastern cats
Weight range	3.5–7kg (8–15lb)
Colours	All self and tortie colours and bi-colours in solid, smoke, shaded, and tipped, and classic tabby pattern
Breed registries	GCCF FIFé CFA TICA TCA (Doll-Faced)

show cats. In North America, the CFA standard describes the Persian as having a "pansy-like" face, a phrase that in my opinion is responsible for many of the eye and nose problems that afflict this breed.

The Persian coat is a chore. The breed's top spot in North America and declining ranking in Europe may reflect national trends for indoor or free-ranging cats.

Often described as a "teddy-bear" coat, the Exotic's short hair has a dense, plush texture that comes from its Persian heritage.

ORIENTAL LONGHAIRS

Get two breeds in a room and you may end up with three names. An Oriental Longhair is the longhaired counterpart to the Oriental Shorthair. In North America it descends from a cross of that breed with a Balinese (the longhaired counterpart of the Siamese). In Britain, the same breed is descended from matings of Siamese and Abyssinians, and before 2003 was called the Angora in the GCCF – although it is not related to Turkish Angoras. In FIFé, the British breed was once called the Javanese to avoid confusion with the Turkish Angora – but that happens to be the name used in North America for some Balinese colours.

EXOTIC

Date of origin	1960s
Place of origin	United States
Ancestry	Persian, American Shorthair
Weight range	3.5–7kg (8–15lb)
Colours	All self and tortie colours and bi-colours in solid, smoke, shaded, and tipped, and classic tabby pattern
Breed registries	GCCF FIFé CFA TICA

COLOURPOINT PERSIAN

The Colourpoint Persian has the build, face, and coat of the Persian with the colouring of a Siamese and was possibly the first deliberate crossing of two breeds. They are regarded as part of the Persian breed by the GCCF and CFA, but a separate breed by some other registries. The body is cobby and carried low on short, strong legs, and the round head has the same full cheeks and short nose as the Persian. The pointed coat is influenced by temperature, and the eyes are generally less intensely blue than in the Siamese. The widely differing personalities of the two parent breeds result in a cat that is more outgoing than the Persian, while more relaxed than the Siamese. The main demand that this breed places on its owner is still the time needed to care for the high-maintenance coat.

Persian cats in Europe still tend to have longer noses than those in North America, where concern about facial health problems has led some breeders to deliberately move away from the mainstream and breed for healthier head shapes.

Over generations, as selective breeding made the face flatter, it also made the coat longer, up to 12cm (5in) long in top show cats. Long coats of fine down demand a considerable investment of time in daily grooming, and this is without doubt why the Exotic is now North America's second most popular breed. The Exotic is the result of an experiment that went wrong. Breeders were trying to produce an American Shorthair with the shimmering coat and green eyes of a silver Persian. Instead they got the Persian in a more manageable short coat. Exotics produce occasional longhaired kittens, but rather than calling these Persians, several registries recognize them as yet another breed, the Longhaired Exotic Variant. The Exotic's soft, plush coat is thicker and somewhat longer than many shorthair coats, and it needs a little additional grooming to keep it looking its best.

Flat-faced Persians and Exotics are popular because their prominent eyes and flat foreheads bring out the parent in us. We're instinctively attracted to that shape. They're like living, cuddly teddy bears. But before acquiring one, get health advice about them from a vet with experience in feline medicine. The Persian and Exotic cat populations have a shorter life expectancy than the general cat population – almost four years shorter – for one profound reason: polycystic kidney disease (PKD). This inherited cause of kidney failure is carried in the genes of approximately 40 per cent of Persians and breeds genetically similar to them. There is a simple gene test for PKD and a simple rule to follow if acquiring a Persian (or Exotic): purchase only from breeders who breed only from lines genetically tested and proven not to carry this disease. Persians also have also a high incidence of retained testicles.

Longhaired Turkish Cats

Longhaired cats from Turkey were extensively used in the creation of the Persian, and by the early 20th century, the original-type Turkish longhair was virtually extinct. The post-Ottoman Turkish government designated these cats a national treasure and, through the Ankara Zoo, established a breeding programme favouring all-white cats with odd eyes, one blue and one yellow. The breed is now known as the Turkish Angora. It has a semi-long coat with little downy undercoat, clothing a lithe body, and remains rare.

The Turkish Van originated as a naturally occurring white cat with orange ears and tail, breeding true in relative isolation in the mountainous Lake Van region of eastern Turkey. Today it is almost extinct in that region, although a breeding programme exists at Van Yüzüncü Yıl University. This bi-colour pattern is now called "van" in any cat from anywhere that is mostly white with coloured ears and tail. The strict colour standards for the breed extend to the eyes, which must be amber, blue, or one of each, the last being the "classic" look for the breed. In Britain, the all-white

The Turkish Angora languished in undeserved obscurity for much of its history. The moderate type and semi-long coat don't look highly bred – which is no bad thing.

These large, handsome cats have become popular, reflecting a desire among owners to have cuddly cats that are, perhaps, like dogs without the walking.

In its homeland the Maine Coon has always been overshadowed by the Persian, but abroad its natural, wild looks are more popular.

first was the Birman (*see* page 27) but by far the most popular, especially in North America and the United Kingdom, is the Ragdoll.

Ragdoll

The name Ragdoll is a registered trademark. Most of the Ragdolls I see at the veterinary clinic genuinely live up to their name and are laid back, relaxed individuals, but I've also known Ragdolls that are neighbourhood thugs, keeping even the local feral cats out of their gardens. One Kuwaiti-born client of mine is particularly proud of how her two Ragdolls efficiently attack a local feral cat (which she's named Saddam) whenever he enters their garden!

The Ragdoll is a relatively large, solid cat, with a long body and a rounded face. The coat is medium length, silky, and flowing, and comes in a mitted pattern, a pointed pattern, and a bi-colour that is similar to the mitted but with more white. Its reputation for being happy to live indoors has helped it gain popularity in regions of Australia where outdoor cats must legally be under your control. A heart condition called hypertrophic cardiomyopathy (HCM) exists within the breed, and there is a genetic test to determine whether individuals carry this gene. An almost identical breed exists in more colours, called the RagaMuffin

RAGDOLL	
Date of origin	1960s
Place of origin	United States
Ancestry	Birman-type cats, white longhaired cats
Weight range	4.5–9kg (10–20lb)
Colours	All self and tortie colours (excluding cinnamon), and bi-colours, in solid and tabby with pointed pattern
Breed registries	GCCF FIFé CFA TICA

Turkish Vankedisi, also sometimes called Van Kedi, is recognized by the GCCF.

Mitted cats

White feet are common within the random-bred cat population, but during the last 50 years several breeds have been selectively bred for this colour trait. The

MAINE COON	
Date of origin	1860s
Place of origin	United States
Ancestry	Farm cats
Weight range	4–10kg (9–22lb)
Colours	Traditional Western self and tortie colours and bi-colours in solid, smoke, and shaded, and in classic and mackerel tabby patterns
Breed registries	GCCF FIFé CFA TICA

to avoid legal problems related to the trademarked name, and is recognized in North America by the CFA.

Cold-climate longhair cats

Let me start with a disclaimer. These northern cats are my favourite longhair breeds: big, robust, level-headed cats, with luxurious coats consisting mostly of heavy, shiny guard hair rather than cotton-candy soft, fine down. They do need more grooming than shorthair cats, but if you make sure you routinely brush and comb behind the ears and the backs of the legs, they don't matt up anywhere near as intensely as Persians do. If these sensible longhaired northern breeds appeal, and you live in northern Europe or northern North America, your local cat rescue organizations may have longhairs needing good homes.

Maine Coon

Rightly popular in North America, the Maine Coon is a big cat – but not as big as some press reports claim. Females in particular are commonly no larger than American cat-average. The thick coat is

BIRMANS, SNOWSHOES, AND TEMPLECATS WEAR MITTENS

Some early Siamese had white toes or other markings, which have been almost entirely bred out over the decades. The Snowshoe has mitted white feet, and was once described as a shorthaired Birman but genetically it was developed in the United States from Siamese carrying the recessive gene for white mitts and American Shorthairs. The Templecat is claimed with more justification to be a shorthaired Birman: it too has mitted paws and was developed in New Zealand using Birmans and Oriental Shorthairs.

In a summer coat, the Maine is more like a shaggy shorthair – in fact it was once called the Maine Shag.

The Wegie is more angular than the square-jawed Maine, and the coarse protective coat has a mane that it keeps all year, even through its heavy summer moult.

of course water-repellent, and my Maine Coon Millie was as attracted to water as a Labrador Retriever, happy to stand chest deep in our pond, dazzled by the sight of fish that she was never able to catch. Originally only the tabbies were called Coons, because of their passing resemblance to raccoons, and tabbies are still valued because they seem to reflect the barn-cat origins of the breed. Although in many ways self-contained, the Maine Coon is often quite vocal, with a distinctive, chirping trill used in greeting. Some individuals carry the gene for hypertrophic cardiomyopathy (HCM), for which all breeding cats should be tested. Others are predisposed both to hip dysplasia and to slipping kneecaps.

Norwegian Forest Cat

Cats came to Scandinavia both by gradual spread from mainland Europe and directly from the Byzantine empire through trade and returning Viking mercenaries. This is why some colours are common in Turkey

Although long hair is relatively unusual in random-bred cats, cats like Wegies are not too hard to find in cold countries. It is, after all, meant to be the distillation of a natural, national type.

NORWEGIAN FOREST CAT	
Date of origin	1930s
Place of origin	Norway
Ancestry	Farm cats
Weight range	3–9kg (7–20lbs)
Colours	Traditional Western self and tortie colours and bi-colours in solid, smoke, shaded, and tipped, and Western tabby patterns
Breed registries	GCCF FIFé CFA TICA

Genetic studies show there are several quite diverse lineages in the Siberian, which is not surprising given its recent recognition and often hazy origins.

and Norway but rare in between, but also how the longhair gene became embedded within the regional population. A long coat offered a distinct advantage in the harsh northern winters, and it became a widespread trait in household and especially farm cats in Norway. By the 1930s the Skogkatt or Skaukatt was regarded as a distinctive breed.

Known to us as the Norwegian Forest Cat, or Wegie, this breed is large, robust, and muscular, reflecting its farm-cat origins. The glossy, smooth top coat covers a dense, insulating undercoat. Like the Maine Coon, the Wegie evolved to survive in a cold climate and enjoys access to the outdoors.

Siberian

Like the other large, longhair breeds, the Siberian is descended from cats that survived in a cold and harsh climate. The type was overlooked until the 1980s, but then spread rapidly, with cats exported to Europe and North America in the 1990s, initially as the Siberian Forest Cat. To avoid confusion with the Norwegian Forest Cat, it was renamed the Siberian. This is a powerful, muscular cat with a heavy-set body and substantial legs. The Neva Masquerade is the Siberian in a pointed pattern – which was recorded over two centuries ago in eastern Russia.

The Siberian has had to differentiate itself from the Maine and the Wegie for breed registries, but for owners health should matter more than such details.

SIBERIAN	
Date of origin	1980s
Place of origin	Eastern Russia
Ancestry	Household and farm cats
Weight range	4.5–9kg (10–20lb)
Colours	Traditional Western self and tortie colours and bi-colours in solid, smoke, shaded, and tipped, with traditional tabby patterns
Breed registries	GCCF FIFé CFA TICA

Chapter 2
A new cat in the family

How cats communicate with us

The longer I've worked with cats, the more I've come to appreciate how easy it is to misunderstand them. Dogs are relatively easy for us to interpret because, companionable and gregarious as we both are, we have in common many ways of communicating. We share similar facial muscles, and we have had generations of experience living with each other. We even wag our butts the same way when we're really happy. Cats have fewer facial muscles, so their faces are more difficult for us to read – but their bodies aren't. Cats have a dramatic variety of ways of telling other cats, or us, to go away.

Cat communication is different

Having a new cat join your family is wonderful, but it's not uncommon for me to meet people with unwarranted expectations of what a cat needs, or what it can do, or how it will behave, especially an indoor cat. Misapprehensions are so common that I have a nurse whose dedicated responsibility is to answer people's questions about why their cats do what they do. So, before going further, this is a good time to go over exactly how and why cats communicate the way they do, with each other and also with us. This is fundamental information and it's at the root of understanding your cat's feelings and emotions, something that's essential if the two of you are going to get maximum pleasure out of sharing a home with each other (*see pages 90-5*).

Touch and scent

At birth, the only developed senses your cat had were heat-seeking, touch, and smell, all used to find first mother and then her nipples and nourishment. Touch and scent continue to play a powerful role throughout life. Adult cats that know each other will use nose-to-nose touch to greet each other – or you. Cats that have grown up together also enjoy body contact when relaxing with each other – or with you.

Every cat has its own unique scent signature in scent glands on its chin, at the corners of the lips, on the top of the head, and at the base of the tail. Washing doesn't just clean the hair and massage the skin. It transfers these glandular scents to the paws and then over the body. And that familiar, calming scent is left on you, or the side of the sofa or a fence post when your cat rubs against it.

It looks like an air-kiss or peck on the cheek, but this sort of close up contact really means something to a cat. It shows a degree of familiarity and trust.

We're inclined to see this leg-rubbing as the closest a cat can get to a hug. The truth is subtly different: our cats are using scent to mark us as "theirs".

Facial scent is so effective in modifying a cat's behaviour that it has been synthesized and marketed as a spray for calming certain behaviours, expecially in multiple-cat households (*see* page 121).

Body language

Along with scent, body language is the second native language of cats. Sometimes feline body language is so subtle and nuanced we miss what cats are saying to each other or to us.

I'm going to break down body language into its component parts here to describe it, but let me explain right now that doing this won't work at home! You can't interpret what a cat is saying by looking *only* at what it's doing with its tail, or its ears, or its voice.

A cat arches its back: is it frightened, upset, or angry? Certainly. A cat arches its back: is it friendly, content, happy to see you? Absolutely. You only know which if you've also read its facial expression, seen its eyes and ears, looked at what it's doing with its hair, listened to what it's saying with its voice. Body language – cat communication – is the sum of all parts.

Cats don't live in packs, so have less need for body language that enhances social togetherness. Social rules are needed only for mating, raising kittens, living in a feral colony of related females, or living in unrelated multi-cat households with us (*see* pages 127–31). The purpose of most body language is to avoid or end physical confrontation. In that context, the eyes, ears, and head are paramount, followed by the body and tail. Vocal communication, so important to us, only backs up all this visual signalling in cats, as do marks that say things when the cat isn't even there.

Cats think it's rude to stare, so they often look and then casually look away. Relaxed but alert, this cat is paying attention to something that has caught its eye.

Expressive eyes

As in all other mammals, dilated pupils accompany excitement in a cat, including excitement associated with fear or aggression – which is why cats I examine usually have dilated eyes. Smaller pupils usually indicate confidence but also confident anger. More subtly, cats look away to resolve potential conflict. Even more subtly, they slowly blink, an effective way to disengage from an aggressive stare from another cat. Adding a yawn to the blink sends an even more powerful message of "no aggro". Try slow blinking when your cat is looking at you. Chances are it might slow blink back then give itself a lick, its way of saying "I'm not threatening either."

Mobile ears

Cats can swivel their ears through a full 180 degrees, as well as raise and lower them. They can even operate each ear independently of the other, perfect for scanning and accurately locating any sound. That's what ears evolved for, but this mobility also makes them ideal for sending semaphore signals to other cats.

- **Forward but held back just a bit:** content and relaxed.
- **Further forward with no tilt:** listening intently.

Flattened ears are out of danger in a fight, and there's no mistaking the fear and aggression here. But the pupils are not fully dilated: this cat is still in control.

QUESTIONS AND ANSWERS

Are cats really attracted to people who don't like cats?

Yes, they are. Cat lovers, or even just cat likers, look at cats. The more you like cats, the more likely it is that you will make prolonged eye contact with them. Cats find a direct stare disconcerting. In silent feline show-downs, the rivals stare at each other until one turns away and the potential conflict is resolved. People who don't like cats are inclined to avoid looking at them. In cat terms, that's interpreted as politeness, so the resident cat goes to socialize with that person first.

- **Slightly back and slightly flattened:** anxious.
- **More flattened:** fearful.
- **Straight back and flat on the skull:** intense fear.
- **Flattened but visibly to the sides:** fearful and aggressive.
- **One ear flattened and the other not:** ambivalent fear.

Scanning whiskers

Cats don't use their whiskers, or vibrissae, just to judge the width of gaps, but also to indicate mood. The whiskers are normally slightly to the side on a relaxed cat, but when something triggers the cat's interest they swivel forwards. When a cat is really excited, these whiskers can extend forward in front of the muzzle. A frightened cat pulls its whiskers right back along its cheeks, making it look smaller and signalling, "I'm not a threat to you."

The whole head and mouth

A contented cat stretches its head forward and up, encouraging a touch.

FOOT STAMPING

When feral cats hiss and spit and flatten their ears back to protect them from the impending fight, they may also stamp a foot. The meaning is obvious to all predators, whatever their size, and even the nastiest will back off. The only individuals I've ever met who don't are people intent on capturing feral cats for neuter and release programmes.

Touch a cat's head in a friendly way, and the chances are it will arch its back, inviting you to stroke along its spine – and pick up its scent on your hand as you do.

That's simple, but other head moves are more ambivalent. An aggressive cat will lower its head, but so will a submissive one. A fearful and defensive cat will raise its head, but so will a confident one. To tell the difference, watch the mouth too. A little bit of visible tongue suggests contentment (unless its tongue is just too big and doesn't fit in) while lip-licking indicates anxiety (or an imminent meal). Remember, cats communicate with their whole bodies, and you need to put the whole package together to decipher what your cat is saying.

Top left *This classic Halloween cat is playing a game of bluff. Whether a resident cat or some other threat provoked this reaction, the posture is designed to say "you don't want to mess with someone my size".*

Top right *This rolling kitten has its claws sheathed and a relaxed face. This playful, slightly ingratiating greeting is a little like a human smile on meeting a stranger.*

Above left *This relaxed cat is using its ears principally for hearing and its tail principally for balance. The very absence of overt signals tells us there is no threat or excitement around.*

Above right *Whatever this cat is staring at so intently, it isn't quite sure whether it is friend or foe. Slightly swivelled ears, an erect, hooked tail, and a hint of crouched readiness all indicate alert caution.*

Body posture

An aggressive cat straightens its hind legs and erects the hair along its spine and tail to look bigger. A defensive cat erects all its hair and stands side-on to the threat to look bigger still. It may walk slowly away, sideways, in crab fashion. Kittens do this when they're playing.

A submissive cat crouches to appear small and unthreatening. It may roll over as a gesture of appeasement, which also gives it the advantage of facing its threat with teeth and all claws. Playful cats also roll over, but keep their claws sheathed and their ears erect. They invite a belly rub, although some feel internal conflict

when stroked on the belly and bite (*see* page 116). Females in season roll wantonly and drag themselves around as if their hind legs are broken, true drama queens in all senses. And of course, cats roll just to scratch their backs.

The tail

A cat's tail is more than just a toy for her kittens to play with, or a rudder, or a counterbalance to the rest of the body. Tail activity has specific meanings.
- **Twitching the tip:** concentration and interest.
- **Faster twitching:** more intense concentration and possible annoyance.

- **Erect and bristling:** fear.
- **Horizontal while walking:** relaxed confidence.
- **Raised when meeting other cat or us:** friendliness or "follow me".
- **Raised with the tip hooked over:** friendly but cautious.
- **Wrapped around another cat or us:** greeting, demanding attention or food.
- **Raised and quivering while hind feet tread:** urine spraying.
- **Raised and quivering without spraying while greeting a person:** "I'm *so* happy to see you".
- **Sweeping from side to side:** ready for action, emotion including anger.
- **Rapid swishing:** extreme excitement, potential aggression but sometimes an invitation to play.

Vocal dexterity

If you are a typical cat owner, you are almost intuitively aware that the cat's miaow is brilliantly expressive. A cousin of mine simply named his cat Mew, the common call of kittens: high pitched as a polite call for help or loud and more frantic as an urgent plea for help. Vocabulary broadens as a cat matures. Adults are more expressive, mewing quietly or even silently for attention, miaowing more emphatically for more attention, MIAOWing! with a command, and MIAOWing! repeatedly when frightened or panicked.

As well as miaows, cats use their voice in a superb variety of ways, most of which are instantly understandable as greeting, grumbling, nagging, and even swearing. Generally speaking, low tones mean displeasure while high tones indicate friendliness and happiness.

- **Grumble or growl:** "back off" warning.
- **Hiss or spit:** extreme warning.
- **Shriek or scream:** fear or high distress, anger or pain.
- **Purr:** contentment, but also done to comfort itself when in pain.
- **Yowl:** used when threatened, but also particularly by Siamese, Oriental, and Burmese type cats as a way of saying "Where is my family?"

It can seem that no other animal relaxes quite so wholeheartedly as a dozing cat. Even the slightly open eyes appear indolent rather than watchful.

TALKATIVE CAT BREEDS

Several years ago I carried out a survey of vets' perception of cat behaviour, and they consistently reported that Persian cats were less vocal than cat average, while Siamese and Orientals were more vocal than average. I don't know for sure if this is so. The respected animal behaviourist John Bradshaw says that cats miaow at us because they are trying to imitate human speech. If that is so, the cats that are most likely to be loquacious are those raised from birth in constant contact with us.

Oriental breeds, such as the Korat, are perceived to be naturally chatty, but perhaps we talk more to a cat that we think will talk back: we may create what we expect.

QUESTIONS AND ANSWERS

Do cats purr just for us?

I've said it before: the cat's purr is a universal sound of peace. Cats purr when happy and content, but they also purr when I take a blood sample or hold them on their sides for an extended ultrasound heart examination. I interpret this type of purr as a way of saying, "I'm co-operating. No need to use forceful restraint."

Cats purr when they are on their own, so purring isn't just for us. From an evolutionary perspective, it must have a significant benefit because it uses energy. In 2009 in the journal Current Biology, it was suggested that cats may actively use a different type of purr, what was called a "soliciting purr", in which they embed a high pitched sound similar to a human baby cry, to get their human's attention. A soliciting purr, according to Dr Karen McComb, is more urgent and less pleasant than an ordinary purr and is used by cats strongly attached to one particular person.

The sneering expression of the flehmen reaction directs scents to a receptor just behind the upper front teeth. It looks peculiar in your cat, but downright alarming in a lion: all members of the cat family share this behaviour.

SNIFFING AND SNEERING

Flehmen, the sniff and sneer reaction, may make a cat look like it feels disgust as it wrinkles its nose, but that isn't the case. Physically, a cat needs to sneer to inhale scent molecules through the top of its mouth to its vomeronasal, or Jacobsen's, organ. This is a scenting organ that cats have but we (and dogs) don't, used for scenting sex. The scent of catnip may also be picked up by the vomeronasal organ.

- **Chirrup:** trill-like sound used as a friendly greeting, especially noted in Maine Coons.
- **Chatter:** sound of frustration, used for example when prey is visible but out of reach beyond a window.
- **Caterwaul:** strident, low moan of a cat wanting sex.

Personal advertising

Cats have evolved ways to communicate with other cats even when they aren't present. Urine and faeces, because they are produced in abundance, are perfect products left to mark territory or solicit for sex. Unneutered tom cats routinely spray their sour, pungent urine at feline nose level, but so do neutered toms on occasion, and even neutered females. In my experience the Siamese is the breed most likely to spray indoors. A neutered

Once one cat sprays, others tend to follow suit in a sort of arms race. Overpowering the smell with one cats dislike, such as dilute citrus or lavender oil, may help.

pet cat urine spraying indoors has not lost its toilet training; spraying is a response to a perceived threat to the cat's territory, and it can be a challenge to overcome (*see* page 130).

Most cats, whether neutered or intact, hygienically bury their faeces in cat litter or outdoors in sand or soil, but some don't. They leave theirs in visible, often prominent spots, such as the middle of a garden path. Their scent-laden faeces acts as a visible territory marker, especially when the resident cat's territory is threatened by another cat. If an indoor

cat dumps, for example, on your bed, again this isn't a loss of house training, it's a cat's way of mixing its scent with yours, to reassure itself of its position in your family (*see* page 128).

Visible markers

When a cat scratches a tree – or more frequently your furniture– it isn't just sharpening its nails and exercising its leg muscles, it's leaving a scent marker. Doormats, which indicate the entrances to both our territories and those of our cats, are frequently scratched to leave visible and odour markers, but highly visible vertical scratch marks are also important. Cats that stand on their tiptoes to leave high scratch marks are advertising how big and strong they are.

The friendly greeting

Your family cat greets you by "smiling" as it approaches you, walking almost on tiptoes as it meets you and rubbing against your leg. We like to call all of that

affection, and I'm sure it is on one level, but what's really happening is your cat is exchanging odours with you and raising its bum, inviting you to sniff it – as you would if you were another cat.

Cats have important scent glands, the anal sacs, on each side of the anus. They anoint each dump they take with this "daily news", information such as when the cat dumped, whether the dumper was a male or female (and if it was a female whether she was ready to mate), and, according to French researchers who have investigated the chemical components of anal sac discharge, at least a dozen more items of information that we simply don't yet understand. Cats will pick up this ever-changing intelligence from faeces, but also directly from sniffing each other's anal sac region. Dogs, of course, do the same amongst themselves.

It means nothing to us, because we can't see it, but a cat rubbing a wall is the feline equivalent of a graffiti artist leaving their '"tag" for others to read.

Above left *Cats like to mark upright objects that are prominent in their territory. To them, the garden bird table and your dining table indoors are much the same.*

Above right *Nose-to-nose contact between friendly cats is often followed by a full-length body rub, ending with the cats nose-to-tail for a good informative sniff.*

GREASY MARKS

Face rubbing on doorways or furniture will, with time, leave a grey-brown, greasy mark. Grease-removing cleanser is effective for removing these dirty marks but remember, your cat will now go into overdrive reapplying its scent marker.

Cats have different personalities

It may be that a red-pigmented cat is more predisposed to jumpiness than a darker individual, but any effect is subtle enough to go unnoticed in everyday life.

Your cat has an adaptable personality that is the result of a variety of factors. Its genetic inheritance, who its parents are, naturally affects personality, which is why there are breed differences in behaviour. But early experiences with its mother, its littermates, and its physical environment are equally (if not more) important. There are other factors, too – there is even a suggestion that coat colour may be associated with personality.

Inherited traits

Studying inheritance of behaviour is complicated. One study of the trait of "boldness" did find that tom cats who were more likely to approach novel objects and people tended to sire kittens with similar fearless or bold personalities. In the same study, timid toms tended to sire kittens that in adulthood were also timid. In another study British Shorthair cats with red coat colour experienced more difficulties when handled by unfamiliar people than cats of the same breed with other coat colours. Doctors know that true red-headed people (with higher levels of the pigment phaeomelanin) are more susceptible to pain than others, and vets know that red-haired Cocker Spaniels are more likely to have "avalanche-of-rage" syndrome than parti-coloured Cockers, but science doesn't know whether coat

colour is strongly associated with a cat's personality. When I surveyed vets asking questions about cat behaviour, they felt there were differences in personality between breeds, but they didn't report personality differences related to colour.

Early learning is vital too

There is not the shadow of a doubt in my mind that genes play a significant role in your cat's personality. A litter of kittens that has shared early experiences still contains a variety of different genes and

Timidity is often learned from a mother – which is why shelters take care to handle the kittens of feral mothers a lot – but may be inherited from the absent father.

Kittens that are played with make the most sociable and playful cats. Lavish the same attention on a moggy and a pedigree kitten, and the adults will be very similar.

so a mix of personalities. Even so, early experiences between two and seven weeks of age are critical for development, and all studies reach the same conclusions here. Being handled often and by different people increases a cat's sociability towards people, and exposure to a variety of sights, sounds, and experiences (such as barking dogs, active children, or car journeys) helps create a calmer, more confident personality.

Introverts and extraverts

For a long time, behaviourists described cats simply as either excitable or timid, but there are many more pairs of opposite terms that also describe your cat's personality. A cat is likely to have characteristics from each list.

Calm	Excitable
Bold	Timid
Alert	Placid
Friendly	Unfriendly
Outgoing	Withdrawn
Active	Passive
Vocal	Quiet
Inquisitive	Uninterested
Sensitive	Insensitive
Affectionate	Distant
Sociable	Antisocial
Assertive	Retiring

Think of your cat in these terms and you'll have a better understanding of its true personality.

The biggest part of a cat's activity budget is in fact pretty inactive. Cats with a lot do tend to sleep less than cossetted pets.

Activity budgets

Your cat's character also manifests itself in how it spends its time. The cat behaviourist Vicky Halls uses an observational tool called an "activity budget" to assess an individual cat's personality, calculating in hours how much time a cat spends on specific activities. The classic cat, the domestic farm cat, will typically have an activity budget like this:

- **Sleeping or resting** 15 hours
- **Grooming and playing** 3 hours
- **Hunting, eating, exploring** 6 hours

CHATTERBOXES

A cat's personality affects how much it wants to talk to you. Some cats have pretty much nothing they want to say, while others are real chatterboxes. Of course, genetics and learning play important roles in talking. Some cats talk a lot because they've discovered it's the best way to get their person's attention.

Vicky has six activities in her pet cat activity budget:
- Sleeping
- Interacting with the indoor environment
- Time spent outdoors
- Socially interacting with other cats or with people
- Grooming
- Eating

This is another neat way to compare personalities, especially if you have more than one cat.

Be prepared

Isn't it fascinating that the world's most successful feline ever willingly enjoys living with the world's most successful primate? It's not just humanized cats, those raised from kittenhood in our homes, that do, but also feral cats with no experience of human contact. Many feral cats feel more secure on defined human territories, where they are more likely to find food, shelter, and safety from larger predators. Whether it is a kitten, a humanized adult, a stray, or a true feral cat, the better prepared you are when a cat enters your home the more enjoyable your lives together will be.

Which cat is right for you?

Moggy or pedigree, kitten or adult, home-reared or feral, male or female, shorthair or longhair? There are plenty of decisions to make before you even begin looking for a cat. Not that all of you will actively go looking: from the statistics I've seen, almost half of you won't be making the decision about what type of cat you'll get or where you'll get it. Cats make that decision for you, either by choosing to join your family or by being born unexpectedly in your neighbourhood, needing a good home.

Be sensible

Do you have hay fever, allergies, or asthma? Are you extremely house-proud? Do you live in furnished rented accommodation? Is money really tight, so tight you have to watch any extra expenses? Does your work mean you're constantly away from home? If you answer "yes" to any of these questions, think very carefully before getting a cat. Have a realistic exit plan in case it doesn't work out – I don't mean for you, I mean for the cat! If you think there may be problems that indicate the cat can't stay with you, you simply *must* ensure that you know the cat will go on to a safe and secure home. To do anything else is downright selfish on your part.

HEALTH CHECKLIST FOR ALL NEW ARRIVALS

Many cats, especially those from conscientious breeders and rescue centres, have had a health check before coming to you. Even so, observe your new cat's behaviour closely, especially during its first 24 hours in your home, and watch for potential health problems. (*see* pages 134–81). If you answer "No" to any of these observations, schedule a visit to your vet the same day or next day:

- Eats normally
- Urinates and defecates without any difficulty or distress
- Has not vomited and has no diarrhoea
- Breathes easily with no discharge, noise or effort
- Has pink gums and no unpleasant mouth smell
- Has a shiny coat without shiny black speckles (flea dirt) in it
- Gets up, moves, jumps and lies down without difficulty
- Is active and alert

The most common moggy is a shorthaired brown tabby, but if you want a special colour or coat you can find quite a range in shelters, or even within one litter.

Age and looks do matter

Your choice of kitten or adult, short- or longhaired, male or female is too personal for me to give you advice. As for the sex of your cat, because most are or will be neutered (a procedure that diminishes behaviour differences), which sex you get is not as important as it is in other animals, such as the dog.

Owned adult cats often arrive litter trained, but using a designated toilet is so instinctive in all cats that most kittens work out what you want with very few early accidents (*see* page 115). Adults do arrive with fixed personalities, while kittens are still malleable and more open to efforts to mould their behaviour to fit your lifestyle. Personally, I get so much fun out of watching the unself-conscious and heroic antics of kittens that they are my selfish preference. Most of the running costs of a cat – food, essential utensils and accessories, annual health checks, and

You may want your cat's bowl to match your kitchen or be personalized, but what your cat really cares about are its size, shape, and surface feel.

boarding – are fixed, but some cats have additional start-up or running expenses. Kittens will need to be neutered, and longhaired cats often need additional professional grooming.

Prepare for your new arrival

Cats like warm, enclosed spaces. A simple bed is fine, but many prefer the igloo type.

Whatever the style, ensure that it's easily washable and place it in a quiet area. Another bed, such as the type that can be suspended from a radiator, for resting in warmth or sunshine is also useful.

Select food and water bowls for their utility, not high fashion. Cats prefer eating and drinking from shallow, saucer-like bowls, which are easier to lick clean without their whiskers touching the sides. Odour-free heavy plastic is good. Stainless steel can be cold to the tongue. Many cats enjoy drinking running water so, although they sound silly, consider a water fountain for your cat. I'll discuss litter and the litter tray in more detail later but as a general rule use odour-free litter and control odour by scooping daily or twice daily. Litter trays vary from simple to spectacular, but plastic trays

BRUCE'S INTRODUCTION TIP

Stroking your new cat, then stroking your resident cat or your dog passively mixes their scents. You can accelerate the spread of "family scent" by actively wiping a soft cotton cloth around the cheeks and mouth of your new cat and then wiping the cloth on household furniture, doorways, even on your other pets. When introducing a new cat, after a few days in your home, swap some of its bedding with some bedding from your resident pets. You can even rub all your pets down with each other's bedding.

Familiarity breeds content as far as animals are concerned, and familiarity of scent is the most important. Do all you can to ensure that your pets all smell like family to each other.

with sides high enough to prevent those cats that are closet landscapers from kicking litter out of the tray are practical. Have one tray for each cat, or one on each floor of your home.

I'll also discuss toys in more detail under training, but start with a table tennis ball, an empty water bottle, and a feather on a string on a rod. For adults in particular get a soft catnip toy.

PARIAH CATS

The most severe problem you may encounter when introducing a new cat into what is already a multi-cat household is that all the residents turn on the newcomer and treat it as a pariah. If it has no escape, it will be viciously attacked. If it can escape to a secure location, for example the top of a high cupboard, it will stay there and not leave even to empty its bladder or bowels. Needless to say, don't under any circumstances allow this to continue. The pariah cat should be rehomed promptly in a cat-free environment.

Kittens and humanized cats from reputable sources

Vets' notice boards and receptionists are a reliable first stop when actively looking for a kitten or cat. Be wary of pet shops. In my experience, most are unhygienic and notorious locations for cats to be exposed to infectious viruses such as cat flu (*see* page 135). I'd be equally suspicious of internet and newspaper ads. Make sure they're from real owners or reliable and hygienic cat shelters, not fronts for cat dealers. The very best cat shelters are wonderful. Unfortunately others, particularly those run by cat collectors, those individuals with a personal obsession for gathering up cats, are dreadful. Avoid them! If you are acquiring a rescued cat, be prepared for what is sometimes a forensic examination on your suitability. Don't be intimidated and do have

A kitten from a reputable source gives you the best chance to mould your ideal cat.

The feral in your yard may become a housecat, but some adult ferals have habits (such as spraying) that make a cared-for life outside more suitable.

your own list of questions ready. Has the cat been examined and certified healthy by a vet? Has it been microchipped, vaccinated, treated for internal and external parasites, and neutered? Has it been housed individually at the rescue centre to reduce the risk of infection? Does it have a known name and was it raised in a family environment, or does it come from a feral background? Has it had a personality assessment? Will the rescue centre continue to give advice on behaviour problems?

Feral cats need extra help

Welcoming a truly feral cat into your home is a challenge. If it comes from a rescue centre, part of the initial stages of humanizing it have already taken place. If it has come through your resident cat's cat flap, it is also partly humanized because it feels sufficiently comfortable to come inside your home. If it has taken up residence in your garden and you are willing for it to become a permanent fixture, you will need extra patience.

Feral cats are frightened of people and initially avoid physical contact with us.

> ### Bruce's tip for calming a feral cat
>
> Feral cats are naturally fearful of big potential predators such as us. One way to accustom them to our words is to leave a radio on, tuned to a talk station. Whether it's a shock jock or not is up to you. Personally, I'd go for the more soothing sounds of an erudite interviewer!

They are also much more likely to carry external and internal parasites and be carriers of feline leukaemia virus and/ or feline immune deficiency virus (*see* pages 135–41), so they need veterinary attention sooner rather than later.

If a feral has occupied a garden shed, start by simply providing food, then food with you hanging around in the garden while it eats. You can gradually move the food bowl, ever so slowly, to where you want it to be.

If you are giving a home to a feral from a rescue centre, restrict it to a safe room – but I'd avoid a dog crate as it may panic the cat. Completely avoid contact between the feral and any other cat until your vet has cleared it of carrying infectious viruses such as FeLV or FIV. In an ideal situation, it is good to have the feral cat separated by

a window or screen from other cats and to feed them within sight and smell of each other. Don't expect a feral cat to ever be anything other than a scaredy cat with other people, but most will relax in your presence given time. Some will eventually even seek out your lap.

Calm and slow works best

Whatever awaits your new arrival – your home, your kids, your dog or your other cat (or cats) – avoid sudden introductions. Other than your kids, don't expect your other livestock to welcome the newcomer with open paws. Your dog might, but your resident cat is unlikely to. Most dogs and cats eventually accept a newcomer, but on some rare occasions they never do. If you find yourself in that situation you may be forced to consider rehoming the new cat.

Opposite *It's a good idea to have your kids feed the cat at first, even if they don't take long-term responsibility, because cats are great at cupboard love.*

Right *Cats can live surprisingly contented lives in a state of truce. There may be occasional vocal grumbles, but without fear or aggression on either side.*

Cat-to-kids introductions

Our kids are obviously small humans to us, but not to cats, especially fearful cats. To them, kids are big animals that stare without blinking, that run and skip and walk with jerky movements, that shriek and squeal, and that suddenly try to grab them. So control your kids. Explain how important it is to be calm, to not expect too much too soon from their new member of the family. It's frustrating for them, not to be able to kiss and cuddle and play with a new cat, but if you want the cat to enjoy their company as much as it will enjoy yours, make sure they all get off to a productive and happy start.

CREATE HOUSE RULES FOR YOUR FAMILY

Life changes when you add a cat to your home. If your household means more than just you, especially if there are kids, write up house rules and post them on the fridge. For example:

- Use Milly's name when calling her to her meals
- Feed her if I'm not back by 7p.m.
- Don't give Milly treats – unless she does something for you first
- Milly is allowed everywhere EXCEPT IN ANY BEDROOM
- Don't move Milly's bed: it stays just where it is
- Be careful with the front door open – she's like a bullet

Cat-to-cat introductions

My general rule is that two cats will learn to live compatibly indoors together, three will probably but not necessarily do so, and adding a fourth almost invariably leads to behaviour problems such as urine marking or fights (*see* pages 127–31). Extravert personalities accept newcomers much faster than introverts. Cautious introverts are more likely to be fearful and aggressive and turn your home into a war zone.

Fortunately, most cats aren't true introverts, and even the classic introvert will enter into a careful but eventually more relaxed state of truce with your new cat, where they simply avoid encounters, tolerate one other, and do no more than smack the other if they unavoidably find themselves passing each other in a hallway. It usually takes no more than three weeks for this to happen.

There is some general advice about what type of new cat is best to bring

BRUCE'S DOMESTIC ARRANGEMENTS TIP

Would you like to eat and sleep by your toilet, especially if you don't flush it? Well, neither does your cat, but this is a common problem that I see. All of the cat's needs – the food bowl, the water bowl, and the litter tray – are lined up together in a neat row. Don't do it. Keep the litter tray accessible, but away from the food and water. Once your cat is routinely using it, you can gradually move the tray to its permanent location.

into a resident cat's home (the opposite gender, neutered, and younger) but my experience is that each situation is unique, and these recommendations apply to populations rather than individuals. Whoever you are introducing, at all costs avoid a fearful, nasty, or violent first encounter. If that pattern becomes established, it's very difficult to change.

BRUCE'S TIP FOR GRADUAL INTRODUCTIONS USING A CAT CARRIER

Use a cat carrier as an alternative to a dog crate for short introductions of your new kitten or cat to your resident dog or cat. Put the newcomer in the carrier and place the carrier on a table or chair, above the eye level of your resident. That avoids forced eye contact. When your resident comes in, reward it for calm behaviour. (*see* pages 96–8). If there is hissing, spitting, or swearing, distract your resident but be careful not to mistakenly reward signs of aggression with attention. Arrange frequent meetings this way, initially every few hours, then try feeding them at the same time. When you feel it is safe, try feeding them both with your new cat out of the carrier at one end of the room and the resident at the other.

The carrier is as much to keep the resident cat out as it is to keep the newcomer in during their first encounters.

Cat-to-dog introductions

Generally speaking, cats get on with dogs faster and better than they do with other cats. Dogs are seen as less competition, and besides, cats naturally rule, and most cats know it!

Cats and dogs use different language, and that mixes dogs up. The cat waves its tail, and the dog thinks it's friendly, so the dog approaches and gets batted. The cat raises its forepaw, and the dog thinks it wants to play, so approaches and gets swiped. Dogs quickly learn that cats are really mixed up and unpredictable. Avoid at all costs the possibility of your cat running away from your dog. That triggers the canine chase instinct, and I've known even the gentlest of dogs succumb to its instincts and kill. Excitable, energetic dogs need careful handling. Schedule introductions after they've had vigorous exercise, and make them sit quietly with the cat in a safe location. If the dog's nose gets swiped, don't punish the cat. The aim of the first meetings is for the dog to learn not to chase or irritate the new family member, and a swiped nose is a quick lesson.

Using a crate

Over the last 20 years dog owners have realized that dog crates are ideal for housetraining a new dog quickly. Cats need little housetraining, but enclosed crates are equally good for introducing a new kitten or cat to your home and your resident feline.

The best crate is around a metre (yard) square and 75–100cm (30–39in) high. They unfold and snap together to create a rigid box with a mesh top and floor. Put a litter tray in one corner of the crate, food and water bowls at the corner diagonally opposite, and a blanket or cat bed beside the water bowl. Place plastic bin liners under the crate, to prevent soiling of the floor, and a blanket or large towel over the top and one side of the crate to make it feel more secure for its resident.

With your new cat safe in its crate, allow your resident to come in. Don't force a meeting. Let it do what it wants, but reward calm behaviour with petting and food. It's a good sign if your resident goes over and sniffs the crate. A kitten will respond with an extended paw; this may provoke a hiss or growl. An ideal time to make introductions is just before

Take no chances at first, but even a dog as feisty as the Dachshund is likely to defer to a cat in the household if introductions are made properly.

your cat's mealtimes. Feed your cat in the presence of the crated newcomer. I'd suggest delaying the regular meal by an hour or more, so that your resident is extra hungry.

Alternatives to a crate

If you don't use a crate for introducing your cat to your home, designate an escape-proof room for it to live in for its first days with you. There should be a good hiding place, a litter tray at one end, food and water at the other, a comfortable bed, and some suitable toys. Close the windows and ensure that your cat can sit at the window and look outside. You want it to get used to its new indoor, and potentially outdoor, territory. Stay with your new cat, ideally sitting on the floor with it, and let it explore where it wants. Control the mother in you: don't fuss and coo and force yourself on it. Don't grab! Let it come to you. Talk gently and move slowly. Kittens and extravert adults take their new home in their stride. Introverts need more gentling along. As long as your new cat eats, drinks, uses the litter tray and sleeps, all will be well.

WATCH THAT LITTER TRAY

You probably already know that dogs can be deliciously disgusting and that cat poo isn't just dessert for some of them – it's foie gras, it's caviar. When introducing a cat into a home already occupied by a dog, make sure the cat's litter tray and its food bowl are out of your dog's way. Feeding your cat on a raised surface, such as a safe ledge, is useful. Making the litter tray inaccessible, perhaps under an upturned cardboard box with an opening only large enough for your cat to enter, is sometimes a useful ploy.

BRUCE'S INSURANCE TIP

If you are as fastidious as a typical cat, you'll have already thought about health insurance. If your cat goes outdoors there are the additional risks of physical injuries, infections from other cats, and parasite infestations. That's why outdoor cats need more veterinary attention and have shorter life expectancies than their indoor cousins. One alternative to taking out a health insurance policy is to find out what the monthly or annual premium is for your type of cat and where you live, and then set up your own savings account and drip feed that amount into the account, earning interest until it's needed.

Will your cat always live indoors?

The answer to whether your cat lives indoors or is allowed outdoors is partly logical and partly cultural. For example, many cat rescue centres and breeders in North America stipulate your cat must not go outdoors before they offer their cat to you. But many cat rescue centres and breeders in Europe stipulate your cat must have access to the outdoors before they offer their cat to you. Some European countries and Australian States stipulate your outdoor cat may not wander more than a set distance from your home, laws that mean your cat is not legally allowed to roam. Aside from these cultural and legal influences, there are pragmatic advantages and disadvantages in living indoors or being allowed outdoors.

Advantages of a cat living indoors permanently:
- The risk of serious injury is drastically reduced, resulting in a longer life expectancy.
- The risk of infectious feline diseases is negligible, leading to a longer life expectancy
- The risk of acquiring external parasites such as fleas and internal parasites such as tapeworms is drastically reduced
- There is increased time for developing a close relationship with people
- You maintain good relations with your non-cat-owning neighbours
- Fewer songbirds are killed
- You are not presented with unwanted gifts of dead prey (with the exception of house mice)

Disadvantages of a cat living indoors permanently:
- There is a greater likelihood of problems due to a cat being overweight or obese through lack of exercise
- Boredom or frustration can lead to behaviour problems
- The risk of damage to indoor furniture and carpets through scratching is increased
- There is always a risk of injury or loss if a door or window is left open and an inexperienced cat escapes
- Indoor litter trays are required, increasing routine maintenance and costs of owning a cat
- Indoor toileting problems, both behavioural and medical, are more likely to occur

A reasonably safe garden undoubtedly enriches a cat's environment. Some dedicated owners catproof their boundaries to provide a private playground.

Will your cat go outdoors?

I didn't plan on letting my cat go outdoors, but Milly bullied me with paw punches and command miaowing, so I let her out under supervision – but only after I'd checked out risks and reduced them. The nearest road was twelve gardens away, so traffic risk was slight; if we were nearer to a road, or worse, there was a more exciting field or woods on the other side of the road, I would not have given in to her pestering. It's your choice with your cat, and up to you to assess the advantages and disadvantages.

Advantages of a cat going outdoors

- Exposure to sun, wind, and rain mean a natural existence
- A more stimulating environment provides more mental challenges
- You get vermin control in your garden
- The cat has an outlet for normal behaviours, such as territory marking
- More physical exercise in a larger outdoor territory results in better body tone and less likelihood of obesity
- Stimulating social contact with other cats is possible

Disadvantages of going outdoors

- There is a risk of road-traffic injuries
- There is a risk of cat-fight injuries
- Life-threatening viral infections can be contracted from other cats
- Routine exposure to fleas and other parasites is unavoidable
- The cat may get lost or be stolen
- The cat may become trapped in a tree, cellar, shed, or vehicle
- There is a risk of poisoning from eating poisoned rodents or skin contamination
- A cat's activities can cause friction with neighbours

BRUCE'S OUTDOOR LITTER TRAINING TIP

To get your cat accustomed to using a particular spot as an outdoor lavatory, spread a little of its used litter in the location where you want it to toilet and remove solids as if it was a litter tray.

If kittens get used to the great outdoors, it can be problematic to restrict them to an indoor life later on.

BRUCE'S TIME-SHARING CAT TIP

If a collarless cat wanders in, vacuums up your cat's food, and makes itself at home on a kitchen chair, don't assume it's a homeless stray. I know many cats that "time-share", living in several different homes without their people knowing it! Owners think their cats are out on the prowl, defending their territory and keeping the local rodent population under control, while in fact they're snoozing away in their holiday villas.

Genuine strays often look unkempt. They may be unneutered, or if neutered may be missing the tip of an ear – a visible sign that they've been captured, neutered, and released. If a cat takes up residence with you, have your vet look for a microchip and check out local notice boards and cat rescue centres for cats that match the newcomer's description. Put a safe collar (elasticated or snap-release) on the stray with an identity capsule containing a note asking "Am I a stray?" with your phone number. Don't be surprised if it takes weeks before a cat's other owner realizes their cat shares two (or more) homes. If it's a time-share cat, work out with the other owner who is responsible for preventative inoculations and parasite control. If it's a genuine stray, get it flea treated and health checked.

Cats may seriously damage small trees by scratching, so consider protecting them with guards, but larger trees will take an area of vertical scratching in their stride.

OUTDOOR ENCLOSURES

Where safety or the law dictates that your cat is not allowed outdoors except under supervision, there are practical (although sometimes expensive) alternatives. Mesh window units that let your cat feel fresh air are commercially available, together with cat tunnels leading from windows or cat flaps to outdoor enclosures, some of which are large enough to enclose shrubs and trees. Check on the internet what's available in your area by searching for "outdoor cat enclosures".

Prepare the outdoors for your cat

If your cat will go outside, you can reduce its desire to wander if you make your garden into such an exciting place it prefers to stay there rather than wander.

Plant buddleia (*Buddleja davidii*) and other flowers that attract stimulating butterflies. Although your cat would certainly find them entertaining, avoid bird tables; you don't want to encourage the death of songbirds.

Plant shrubs that will provide shade in hot weather and give cover for your cat. Keep your groundcover planting dense in the flowerbeds, ensuring there's no visible soil to use as a toilet, while encouraging your cat to use a specific area as a toilet by turning it into a finely raked natural tray.

If you don't have a fence, add a few ornamental wooden fence posts around your perimeter on which your cat can perch and survey its surroundings. They also make ideal visible markers for scratching. On the other hand, if you have trees that you don't want your cat to climb, consider wrapping the trunks 1.5–2m (5–6ft) above the ground with a smooth collar around 50cm (20in) wide to make climbing difficult or impossible. Of course, leave a bowl of water outdoors in case your cat is thirsty, but reserve feeding for indoors.

Cats live in three dimensions. Inside, they are limited to chairs, or maybe tables and cupboard tops, but outdoors they can really enjoy looking down on the whole world.

A cat raised with white hamsters may not prey on white hamsters, but any other colour or type of small furry animal will be fair game in its mind. Instincts die hard.

BRUCE'S TIPS TO MINIMIZE OUTDOOR RISKS

It's dangerous in the exciting outdoors, but there are practical ways to reduce the risks.

- Train your cat to come when called (*see* page 101)
- If you are worried, train your cat to wear a harness and lead before you take it outdoors (*see* pages 108–9)
- Initially let your cat out only before meals, when it is hungry and has good reason to return inside promptly
- Microchip your cat and attach visual ID to a collar with a safety release in case it snags
- Neuter your cat: neutered cats wander less (*see* page 141)
- Maintain inoculations against preventable diseases (*see* pages 135–7)
- Use regular protection against fleas, ticks, and other external and internal parasites (*see* page 141)
- The dark hours are most dangerous. In particular, cats are dazzled by headlights and may freeze in the middle of the road. If your cat is out at dusk – and it's better that it's not – ensure that it wears a reflective collar
- Remove any toxic chemicals or plants from where your cat has access

LIVING WITH OTHER FURRIES

Protect any small mammals – gerbils, hamsters, mice, rats, guinea pigs, even fierce buck rabbits – from your new cat. Kittens that are introduced to small mammals at a very young age (between three and seven weeks) are unlikely to chase and kill those mammals when they are mature. But assume that all other cats will naturally do so.

Permanent identification

Have your cat microchipped before letting it outdoors. The microchip is a radio transponder the size of a rice grain, injected by your vet under the skin on the top of the cat's neck. Cat's rarely resent the injection, and certainly object far less than dogs do. A chip is essential if you want to travel abroad with your cat, but it can do more than just identify a lost cat. The type of microchip I use at my clinic includes a thermometer, so I take a cat's temperature simply by waving the scanner over its back. (Ten out of ten cats tell me this is how they would choose to have their temperatures taken if they could.) A microchip can even be used to operate a cat flap.

As well as a microchip I recommend that cats should also carry visible ID, either an engraved tag or a lightweight capsule attached to the collar containing information on paper. A safe collar must have either a very stretchy elasticated section or a snap that releases when a degree of tension is applied. That ensures

that your cat won't get caught if the collar gets entangled in branches.

Self-operating cat flaps

If your cat goes outdoors it needs a way to get back in quickly when you're not there. A regular cat flap is fine, but I'd suggest two alternatives to prevent other cats from using it: a flap operated by a magnet on your cat's collar or, preferably, one that opens only when it picks up the radio signal emitted by your cat's microchip.

Start by holding the flap open and gently guiding the cat through. Graduate to holding it partly open so your cat feels the flap on its back as it slips through. Finally show it how to operate the flap on its own by pressing its head against it. Using food rewards helps (*see* pages 98–9).

Modern collars have snap catches that release under a certain amount of strain. This is far safer for the cat than the old buckle types.

OUTDOOR TO INDOOR LIVING

If your new adult cat has previously led an active outdoor life but will no longer be able to do so because of where you live, it may develop "cabin fever" in its new home and become destructive (*see* pages 122–4). It will need much more play activity with you, as well as interactive play toys to keep its mind and body active when you're not available for play. In almost all circumstances when a cat retires from an outdoor life to one indoors, you need to decrease its food intake. Reduce intake by 10 per cent to start with, and if weight is still gained reduce it by another 10 per cent.

Good nourishment

Cats love fresh meat for sensible reasons. While a dog can survive by scavenging roots, berries, and vegetation, a cat dies if it doesn't eat meat. Cats cannot break down certain essential amino acids and fatty acids found in vegetable matter, only those found in mammals, birds, reptiles, and fish. The best pet food manufacturers understand the cat's unique nutritional requirements and ensure more than adequate levels of these essential nutrients.

A healthy diet is one of the biggest responsibilities we bear for our cats. Doing our best for them means understanding their particular nutritional needs.

Essential nutrients

Animal fat contains essential fatty acids (EFAs), such as arachidonic acid and linoleic acid, that a cat is capable of breaking down or "desaturating". The cat cannot manufacture these nutrients itself. Arachidonic acid is essential for blood clotting, reproduction, and coat condition, while linoleic acid is vital for growth, liver function, and wound healing. A cat's natural diet of small rodents and birds contains a good balance of these essential nutrients, as well as essential amino acids such as taurine and arginine. So does fish, which

Outdoor cats often supplement their diet with prey. You rarely need to adjust the diet if you see this: active hunting cats are not highly prone to weight gain.

BRUCE'S TUNA TIP

While fish is a good source of nutrients for your cat, a tuna-only diet is potentially lethal. Tuna is at the top of the ocean's feeding chain, so it contains high levels of man-made pollutants. But more importantly, tuna also contains an enzyme called thiaminase, which destroys the B vitamin thiamine. This can lead to a painful, life-threatening condition called pansteatitis. Fresh or tinned tuna is perfectly safe as part of, but not all of, your cat's diet.

Left *Dry food or "kibble" of varying shapes can help to scrape tooth surfaces clean, and the pressure of crunching the pieces strengthens tooth roots.*

Below *Wet food is physically similar to a natural diet, complete with meaty smells, so most cats enjoy it. Owners tend to be less keen, although single-serving sachets have more recently become popular.*

is not a natural diet for cats but is an extremely good one.

Home cooking

Your cat will probably love you even more if you cook fresh food daily for it. There is information on home cooking on the internet, but none of what I've read meets my minimum standard of reliability so personally, while I give cats fresh meat (and bones), their main diet is a combination of high-quality wet and dry manufactured cat foods. Take care if you are giving your cat raw meat. As well as the obvious risk of salmonella bacteria in raw poultry, there is the additional risk from the protozoan parasite that causes toxoplasmosis. Eating undercooked or raw meat is the most common way that humans contract toxo, but we can also contract it from cat faeces during the weeks after a cat first consumes this parasite (*see* pages 138–40). Bone-rich food such as a cooked chicken neck is an excellent source of nourishment and provides exercise for the teeth and gums, but take care, especially with voracious or competitive eaters.

Commercial food varieties

Dry food is prepared by cooking then drying under pressure and spraying with fat to add stimulating odours that increase palatability. A preservative must be added to prevent that fat from spoiling. Wet foods are cooked, heat-sterilized, and sealed in sachets or tins. Because wet foods are vacuum-sealed, preservatives aren't necessary. Nutritionally, one type of diet is no better than the other. Dry food gives the teeth and gums more exercise, so it may slow down the development of gum disease. It is popular because it can be left in the bowl all day for your cat to graze on – and cats enjoy grazing – and it can also be used as hidden treats in

COMPARING FOODS

Comparing the protein or fat level of one diet to another takes a little work, because each diet contains a different percentage of water. The only accurate way to compare diets is on a dry-weight basis.

A typical wet food label may say:
Crude protein   8 per cent
Crude fat   7 per cent
Ash   2 per cent
Fibre   1 per cent
Moisture   82 per cent

Taking out that 82 per cent of water leaves 18 per cent of dry matter. To calculate the nutrients in this, multiply the nutrient percentage by 100, then divide it by the dry matter percentage. So for protein in this food, the calculation would be:
8 x 100 = 800, and 800 ÷ 18 = 44.4 per cent

activity toys or in paper bags, for your cat to actively search and find.

The cheaper commercial foods usually have set levels of calories, protein, and fat, but vary the ingredients used at any time to meet these. More expensive foods, usually called "premium" and "super-premium" are made to fixed formulas, always using exactly the same ingredients. Even more exacting recipes are used for a variety of veterinary diets, nutritious foods for the prevention or treatment of certain diseases.

Needs vary by breed and age
Growing kittens have higher energy demands than typical adults, so kitten foods contain higher levels of vitamins and minerals and more protein than diets for adult cats. At the opposite end of the spectrum,

If your cat eats mostly or entirely wet food, it may seem to drink little or nothing, but you should always keep a bowl of fresh water available.

MILK CAN CAUSE DIARRHOEA

Cats love milk and cream, but dairy products occasionally cause diarrhoea. That's because kittens produce an enzyme called lactase to digest lactose, the sugar in milk, but some adult cats don't. They don't have enough of the right bacteria in their intestines to do so. If milk upsets your cat's digestion and causes diarrhoea, offer it either "cat milk" or lactose-free milk for humans lacking the same enzyme, both of which are available from large supermarkets and specialist shops.

controlled diets euphemistically labelled as "neutered cat" or "indoor cat" foods.

Special diets for medical conditions

Some cats are genetically predisposed to develop a variety of urinary problems, lumped together under the name lower urinary tract disorder (LUTD). This is more likely to develop in overweight, lazy, indoor, tom cats that eat dry food. It causes pain or life threatening urinary blockage (see pages 170–1). When dry foods first became popular in the 1970s,

I saw a virtual epidemic of LUTD, simply because several dry-food makers got their formulas wrong. LUTD is no longer as prevalent as it once was. Good manufacturers formulate to prevent it and produce additional "urinary diets" for those that develop it. They also produce "renal diets" for cats with age- or breed-related kidney failure (see page 175), together with various other wet and dry veterinary diets to help cats lose weight, recover from serious illness or surgery, or overcome gastrointestinal disturbances.

older cats need more cellular protection, so cat food makers increase the levels of free-radical scavenging vitamins and minerals in their diets. They claim that their "senior" diets are also more digestible. Longhaired cats, because they swallow more hair while grooming themselves, are more prone to hairballs than other cats. Several manufacturers have responded by formulating diets that help move hair through the stomach and intestines. And because most indoor cats are relatively inactive and neutered, and tend to gain weight, manufacturers now market a variety of calorie-

Kittens use vast amounts of energy to fuel all that growing and their high levels of activity. Get the feeding right now, and your kitten can carry its youthful vigour into a long and healthy adult life.

BRUCE'S BONES TIP

Gum disease is the most common reason why I'm obliged to anaesthetize cats; I have to, in order to attend to their rotten teeth. Most tooth and gum disease can be avoided if a cat learns early in life to eat bones. I started my kitten on chicken bones at eight weeks of age. There are possible drawbacks. Raw chicken bones may carry salmonella bacteria, potentially dangerous to your cat and to people. A raw or cooked bone might get caught between the teeth in the roof of the mouth. Very, very rarely in my experience (in fact I can't recall an incident in the last quarter century), a cat will try to wolf down bones in a dog-like manner and may develop a blockage. This is exceptional, and to me, the benefits from a cat gnawing on bones vastly outweigh the risks

Grooming and hygiene

Cats are magnificent self-operators, wonderfully fastidious with their personal hygiene. I'm sure this is one of the chief reasons why we not only let them share our homes but downright enjoy letting them spend lounge-lizard lives lolling on their backs on our furniture, even our beds, doing zip and just watching time pass by. Cats groom and clean themselves very efficiently, but even so all of them need extra help from us from time to time, especially longhaired and older cats.

Cats groom themselves

A typical cat spends over ten per cent of its time grooming itself. That's about two and a half hours each day; do you spend that much time on your personal hygiene? Grooming is very ritualized – it's a hard-wired genetic trait. Your cat will first lick its coat all over, removing dead hair and superficial debris. Then it will lick its paws and apply cleansing and antiseptic saliva over its head and face, regions it can't reach with its tongue. Grooming cleanses the skin but it also spreads the personal smell from glands over the whole body, so that the cat can leave it on scent posts such as doorways and furniture.

The cat's barbed tongue is highly efficient at removing dead hair and skin cells. One drawback is that quite a lot of that is then swallowed, leading to hairballs.

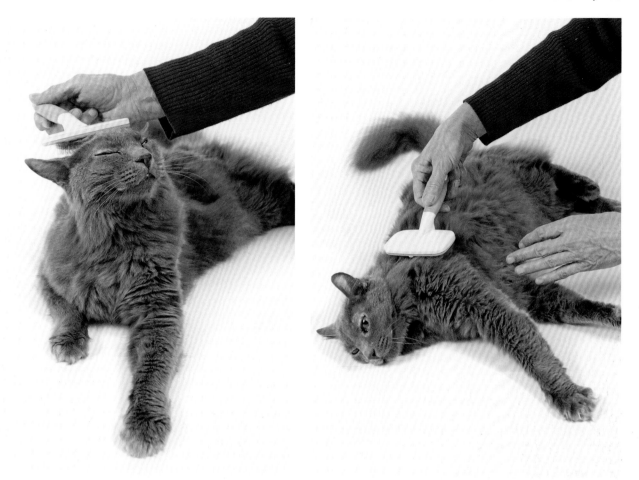

It's easy to help them

Regularly grooming your cat serves two functions. The obvious one is to help your cat maintain a healthy coat and give you a daily opportunity to check all its body openings and its general state of health. The less obvious function of grooming is to enhance the relationship between the two of you. Carried out sensibly and sensitively, grooming your cat is a natural way for you to reinforce your "maternal" role in its life. Pet cats are life-long kittens, and one of the characteristics we usually want to perpetuate in them is a life-long willingness to see us as its mother, the protector and the provider.

As a vet, I also have a personal and vested interest in your routinely grooming your cat, because cats that are accustomed to being groomed and physically inspected by you are more willing to be examined by me. The easier a cat is to examine, the faster I can come up with the diagnosis of a problem.

PERSIAN TYPES NEED EXTRA GROOMING ATTENTION

Cats with flat faces or particularly fine, long hair need daily grooming. This is to prevent the build-up of crusting eye discharge in the nasal folds, or mats of hair that soon become impossible to comb out.

Above *If you accustom your cat to grooming at an early age, when it is still used to being groomed by its real mother, it can be a pleasure rather than a struggle.*

Below *A "slicker" brush with wire pins in a soft cushion is helpful for removing tangles from long coats before they become impenetrable mats.*

Rubber hound glove

Round-toothed comb

Claw clippers and file

Bristle and pin brush

Basic grooming

Start grooming your cat on the first day it arrives in your home. Different coats need different tools and treatment.

For short, smooth coats, use a bristle brush, chamois, or even a hound glove to remove debris and stimulate the skin's glands. A semi-long coat needs twice-weekly brushing with a bristle or slicker brush, followed by combing the long hair with a wide-toothed comb. Longhaired cats need this done daily. Mats are most likely to develop behind the ears and elbows and between the hind legs. Tease mats loose using talcum powder or cornflour, then brush and finally comb through. Be very, very careful if you have to cut out knots with scissors. Cat skin is extremely thin; I sew up inadvertently cut skin several times every year.

WASHING YOUR CAT

A cat only needs wet washing if its coat has become contaminated and can't be cleaned with a dry shampoo. It's a rare cat that accepts a wet shampoo, but if needed, brush first to remove tangles and use a non-slip rubber mat in the bathtub to prevent accidents. Make sure the water is not too hot, and apply the recommended shampoo, avoiding the eyes. Many therapeutic shampoos need to remain on the hair and skin for five very long minutes. Rinse off with either a hand-held shower or containers of tepid-warm water. Towel dry or, if your cat is not frightened by the noise, use a hand-held dryer set at cool or warm, but never hot. Be generous with offered rewards – not that a cat being washed will take them!

BRUCE'S ANAL SACS TIP

Indoor cats are more likely to develop blocked anal sacs that those permitted outdoors. They try to empty them through vigorous and constant anal licking. If help is needed from you, have another person hold your cat and wear disposable gloves. Lift the tail straight up with one hand and place the thumb and forefinger of your other hand at the four- and eight-o'clock positions on either side of the anus. Squeeze firmly but gently, up and towards you, with your fingers ending up at three and nine o'clock. Aim carefully: the stuff that comes out is disgusting.

You are unlikely to be as lucky as this with your cat: a struggling armful of fury is far more common. Fortunately, this is a rare event in any cat's life.

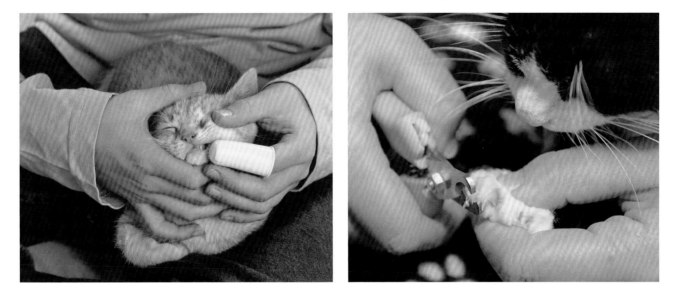

Routine care for teeth and gums

Bad breath usually means gum disease. In young cats, this may be associated with a virus infection early in life (*see* pages 158–9) but in all cats, young and older, it is more often the result of gum inflammation (gingivitis) and infection as a result of poor mouth hygiene.

Routinely check your cat's mouth for odour or foreign material. Gums should be uniformly pink with no added redness where they meet the teeth. Teeth should be white, with no plaque or visible red gum growing onto them.

The easiest way of maintaining a cat's tooth and gum hygiene is to allow the cat do it itself by chewing on bones. The alternative is brushing your cat's teeth, possible if you start training in kittenhood with a small soft toothbrush. An alternative to conventional brushing is to apply an oral antiseptic gel, formulated specially for cats, each day, using a special finger cot that can also massage the gums.

Inspect the eyes, ears and nose

Very long-faced breeds like the Siamese tend to accumulate mucus in the corners of their eyes, while flat-faced breeds are prone to tear overflow. Clean both using dampened cotton wool. Cleanse dark, crusty nasal discharge, also with dampened cotton wool. Check the ears for wax or debris. Surplus clear, colourless wax is not uncommon in indoor cats and can be removed with a cotton bud, but take care. Used incorrectly a cotton bud can act like a plunger, pushing a plug of wax deep into the ear. Ear mites, common in kittens, create gritty, sandy debris. Your vet can give you an effective treatment.

Trim the claws

Most cats don't need their claws clipped until they are older, naturally maintaining sharp claws by themselves. They remove old redundant material by clawing scratching posts or by simply chewing it off. If you want to keep your cat's claws blunt to protect your furniture, you will need to clip them every two weeks.

Press gently behind each claw to extend it. Position a guillotine-type clippers at right angles to the claw, in front of the visible pink "quick" inside the nail material, and squeeze firmly, cutting across the claw. This is painless; it only hurts if you cut into the living quick. I'd suggest replacing cheap clippers every six to nine months, to ensure sharpness.

Above left A finger brush is often the easiest option for brushing a cat's teeth, because you can feel what you are doing better than you can with a conventional long-handled toothbrush.

Above right If you feel nervous about clipping claws, ask your vet to demonstrate first. With time and plenty of treats, most cats will accept you carrying out this task for them, especially if you start when they are young.

Even cats that have attended to their own nail hygiene all their lives need help when they are older. Left unattended claws, particularly dewclaws, can grow into the pads and cause painful abscesses. If your cat won't let you clip its claws in one room try another place. It is less likely to object when it's in a strange environment, which is why it is usually easier at the vet's than it is at home.

BRUCE'S BODY LANGUAGE TIP

Keep grooming sessions short and watch your cat's body language. If the tail starts lashing it's time to stop, even if you haven't finished. Once your cat is used to short sessions, gradually extend them, always giving constant rewards.

Travelling and moving home

With the exception of outgoing extraverts and those that were accustomed to travel at an early age, most cats prefer to stay at home when you and your family go away on holiday. Moving home is another matter. This is a risky time, when indoor cats may wander away in the commotion of moving and outdoor cats become confused and even lost in their new territories. Plan ahead to reduce risks.

Most cats are stay-at-homes

If you're going on holiday, you can put your cat in a well run cattery or, as most cats prefer, you can arrange for it to stay in its own home, either with a cat- (and house-) sitter who moves in, or a neighbour or professional cat visitor arriving once or twice each day to empty the litter tray, fill up the food and water bowls and play with your cat. Gregarious personalities will need additional amusement if they are at home alone.

Your vet can help you find temporary accommodation for your cat; they usually know good catteries and reliable cat-sitters or visitors.

Moving home

Moving home is a different matter. Speaking from my experience, the safest and most pragmatic arrangement is for your cat to spend a few days at an approved cattery from before you move until a few days after the move. By that time you've got your furniture in place and know exactly where your cat stuff will be. That way there's no chance of escape or loss.

If that isn't possible, either get out the crate you used as a kitten pen, or select a small, safe room in your home (from which you've already removed the contents, so the movers don't have to go in it) and use that to protect your cat during the move. Set up the crate or room as you did when your cat arrived, with litter tray, food and water bowls, bedding, and toys.

PET TRAVEL DOCUMENTS

While an up-to-date vaccination certificate and proof of parasite treatment is usually all that is needed to visit a cattery, more complicated and expensive documents are needed if you plan to visit or move to rabies-free regions such as Hawaii, Australia, New Zealand, Sweden, the United Kingdom, or Ireland. Health officials have a habit of changing regulations, so always check the relevant government's website before you travel, but in most instances a cat must be microchipped, vaccinated against rabies, and have a blood sample taken a few weeks later that confirms protection.

A varying interval follows before your cat can visit the region: you will have to wait four months for Hawaii, but six months for many other countries. Read the small print for any quirks in each region's other regulations. For example, Hawaii completely prohibits the import of Bengals, for either short visits or permanent residence!

Pet passports avoid the stress of quarantine, but getting one does take quite a bit of organization beforehand – more than for your own passport.

A move is stressful for everyone, but at least you know where you are going and why. In a cattery, your lucky cat will miss all the chaos and hard work.

Moving day and after

Before the movers arrive, ensure your cat is in its safe place. For the journey, your cat goes with you, not with the movers! It might sound self-evident, but some of my otherwise intelligent clients have sent their cats in a carrier with the delivery van. The cat carrier you use to take your cat to the vet should be fine for the move. Give a light meal, or no food if you know your cat is a poor traveller. If it's a terrible traveller, your vet can provide something to ease the journey, from motion sickness medication to synthetic cheek-gland scent spray to use in the transport carrier.

When your cat arrives in your new home, either with you or from the cattery after you've started to settle in, restrict it to a single room until it wants to investigate its new home. Some cats take weeks to settle in, while others want to explore outdoors immediately – but take care. There are new and unexpected dangers outside. Sprinkle a little of your cat's urine-soiled litter close to your new home to act as an outdoor signpost for its new home, and personally escort your cat outdoors on the first few visits. It usually takes several weeks before a cat becomes fully accustomed to its new indoor and outdoor territories.

BRUCE'S IDENTITY UPDATE TIP

A house move is the time when your cat is most likely to go missing, either because it knows something is up and can't be found before the move, or because it forgets how to get back to its new home when exploring at the other end. In either case, a microchip is invaluable for reuniting you with your lost pet – but it's surprising how many people "fit and forget", so the microchip record contains their previous address. Update your cat's details promptly, and make sure the new owners of your old house have your number – if you haven't moved far, your cat may go "home".

You need to know exactly where your cat is at all times during a move and for some days after, until it accepts that its new home really is home now.

Chapter 3
Cats are trainable

Cat culture

It is certainly true that your cat's ancestors were solitary hunters, loners that marched to their own drumbeat, but your cat differs from them in vital ways. Whether feral or raised with humans, modern cats are much more sociable than wildcats. Because of their enhanced sociability they are relatively easy to "obedience" train: they can be trained to come on command, to sit or to give a paw. Cats respond well to rewards, but don't expect your cat to be willing to race through an obstacle course the way a dog does. A cat's emotions and intelligence are just not the same as those of more gregariously sociable species such as dogs. It is quite easy to train your cat, but successful training depends on understanding your cat's feeling and emotions.

Perpetual kittens

I've mentioned it before but here it goes again, your cat is really a kitten, a Peter Pan character caught forever in feline childhood. The traits we love most in our cats – their playfulness with us, their dependency upon us, their friendliness with their human (and canine) family and their downright cuteness – are all juvenile behaviours that we have perpetuated into their adult lives through selective breeding and early learning. Beneath these characteristics, however, our cats' emotions are not very different from those of their wild ancestors in Africa. What domestication and early learning both do is modify your cat's responses to those emotions.

As wildcat kittens mature, they move apart and defend separate territories. Our cats have smaller territories, and may defend only a favourite spot in the sun.

What is intelligence?

People frequently tell me how intelligent (or for that matter how dumb) their cats are, but I have a problem. I really don't know what cat owners mean when they use words like "intelligent" or "dumb".

Behaviourists are more precise. They describe different forms of intelligence, and each species (and individual) has more, less, or even none of each type. For example, humans are described as having eight different types of intelligence:

- Linguistic
- Logical or mathematical
- Musical
- Spatial
- Bodily or kinesthetic
- Naturalist
- Interpersonal
- Intrapersonal

My hunch is that when people use the word "intelligent" in the context of their cats they mean either "trainable", in that the cat has been easy to train or has efficiently and rapidly trained its owners, or "sensible", in that their cat doesn't do dumb things.

I think that the only accurate way to compare the intelligence of one cat with another is to examine their abilities within different categories of feline intelligence, such as the following five.

- **Spatial intelligence:** the capacity to mentally map comparatively large hunting territories.
- **Bodily-kinesthetic intelligence:** an understanding of motion and forces, and an understanding of mechanics, such as how much propulsion is needed to jump onto a fence.
- **Naturalist intelligence:** an ability to choose the best place to live for safety and for reproduction; an acute understanding of what is dangerous, what to do in self-defence, and how to be properly cautious; and the ability to

Knowing when to patrol your neighbourhood, what's the best vantage point to use, and how to get (and stay) up there are typical feline forms of intelligence.

CATS CAN FEEL GRIEF

When someone – another cat, a dog or a person – is no longer present, because that individual has either died or simply left home, the absence of the familiar can and does cause sadness for some cats. The resulting changes in routine may cause frustration or worry to others. And sometimes the severing of an attachment causes what I have no difficulty in calling grief. A cat's feeling of grief can be a combination of loss, frustration, worry, and bewilderment. Whatever the specific feelings, a grieving cat can become withdrawn, or it may instead become over-attached, following you from room to room, vocalizing and demanding your attention. This may not be the same as grief in human terms, but it is still grief at a loss.

Innate differences in temperament mean certain breeds or individuals really are more laid back or friendly than others, but much is still down to early learning.

CATS DON'T FEEL EMBARRASSMENT

If a cat tries to jump onto something and fails, or accidentally falls off of something, it will usually just get on with life, either trying again or moving on. Some cats sit down and wash themselves after making a mistake, and I've heard it said that this is how they show embarrassment, but that's not right. Grooming after an accident such as a fall is no more than cat body language, telling other cats, or potential predators that the world continues to rotate and nothing much has changed.

know and remember what should and should not be eaten.

- **Interpersonal intelligence:** an innate understanding of the behaviour of other animals, including the ability to predict their likely behaviour from their initial actions; an intuitive inclination to patrol, investigate and mark a territory; and a recognition of the role and importance of kinship, especially the maternal relationship.
- **Intrapersonal intelligence:** an ability to maintain personal hygiene.

Instinctive feelings

Cat intelligence is a composite of all of these abilities, and harnessing that intelligence – training your cat to give you a high five, or to come when its name is called, or to walk on a harness or not to attack passing ankles – depends on your understanding your cat's intelligence, but also its feelings and emotions.

This is where we inevitably make mistakes, because we virtually can't help but project human motivations onto our cats' behaviours. Virtually every day, a cat owner tells me that their cat did something – urinated on the bed, wouldn't allow itself to be petted when the owners came back from a holiday – "to get even". No! That's not true! And to explain why it's not true, we need to understand the cat's basic emotions.

Bedrock behaviours

Your cat's behaviours, feelings, and emotions are both instinctive, which means hard-wired in their brains, and learned. Learning is mostly passive, absorbed from a cat's day-to-day experience. For example, a cat's instinctive response to a dog charging towards it, or to the sudden sound of a vacuum cleaner, is to run away. But if it learned as a kitten that the dog was just a jerk that wanted to play or that the vacuum cleaner wasn't roaring before eating it, without any training from us, the cat learned to control its natural response, which is to fight or to flee. Of course, learning can also be active, as I described when explaining how to introduce your cat to a resident cat or the family dog (*see* pages 67–8). Your cat's basic behaviours – the choice of fight or flight, and the drives to eat and breed –

Left *When your cat rubs against your legs, it isn't "just" marking you with its scent; it is happy that you're there to be marked, enjoying its emotional connection with you.*

Below *Even grooming can be a source of pleasure if it recalls sensations of maternal grooming in your cat.*

are its basic instincts. Colouring each cat's instincts are individual variations on what I consider to be nine basic feelings or emotions they share with us:

- Contentment, happiness, pleasure, or satisfaction
- Elation or euphoria
- Fear, trepidation, or worry
- Anger or rage
- Frustration
- Jealousy
- Desire or lust
- Sadness or depression
- Disgust

Just because we both share these feelings or emotions with cats doesn't mean they are exactly the same in both species. They are not – they are much simpler in cats than in people.

Contentment or happiness

Call them what you will, these feelings are associated with the release of oxytocin and dopamine, the body's "feel-good" brain chemicals. Eating makes your cat feel good. So does being petted or lying in warm sunshine, or playing with a toy or falling asleep on your lap.

Happy and contented cats show affection by playing with us and allowing us to groom them. I'm quite happy to use the word "love" to describe the feeling of attachment some cats have to their owners (remember I said emotions are not exactly the same in both species). Love is a type of attachment that improves the survival prospects of the lovers, and science shows we're both healthier when there's a loving relationship between us.

Elation or euphoria

Cat owners use different descriptions to describe what might be called elation, for example "the mad dash" or "the wall of death". One of my cats would leave her starting gate at maximum speed, race down the hall, hit the bathmat, skid into the bathtub, then walk back into the living room with a "Hi guys. What's up?" look on her face. Some individuals explode with a burst of euphoric activity after using the litter tray. "Yes! I've dumped! I feel great!"

These short episodes of activity may simply be physical manifestations of pleasure or happiness, but to me they represent the release of pent up emotion; they are often caused by a lack of more natural outlets for activity.

When feline strangers or rivals meet, their approaches are usually cautious or tense. And aggressive stance does not mean a cat fight is inevitable.

Fear, trepidation or worry

I see this emotion in cats several times every day, as they refuse to leave their cat carriers for me to examine them. These feelings give a cat thinking time, time to assess how real the potential danger is. Most cats I see will decide their fear is unwarranted within a minute, and leave the cat carrier to investigate the examination room.

Anger or rage

Anger is different from fear. Some cats fear being handled by me but others are angered. Anger is a bad mood, and the angry cat remains angry even after whatever made it angry has been removed. I know one cat that, minutes after my examining it, walks back and bats my leg with his paw.

Rage may appear to be no more than an extension of anger, but neurologists have discovered that rage is intimately linked to the pleasure centre in the cat's brain, with the result that an overflow of pleasing sensations can trigger a rage response. A typical example is lashing out while being petted, a behaviour that is not triggered by fear.

Frustration

Frustration is slightly different. In my experience, one of the most common physical signs of frustration in cats is the teeth chattering of the indoor cat watching potential prey outdoors through a window. In other circumstances a cat will vent its feelings of frustration through aggression. Some cats, having lost a fight with another cat (or the vet) will go home and lash out at the other resident cat or the owner. Just like angry cats, frustrated cats need time to calm down, as well as stimulating environments to prevent frustration.

Jealousy

Scientists tell us that even pigeons experience jealousy, so it's no surprise that this is a basic feline emotion. Sulking is a variation of jealousy. Jealousy is not as common in cats as it is in dogs – our dogs quite commonly and openly say "Pay attention to me, me, me!" when you show interest in another dog – but it is a subtle emotion. A jealous cat might intimidate another cat, or person, who has received attention from the jealous cat's person.

Desire or lust

The urge to mate (less technically known as desire or lust) is triggered in cats by odours, especially those captured by the vomeronasal organ in the roof of the mouth (*see page 56*). It is also triggered by body language – it's impossible to mistake

Extreme fear and anger are joined in the "fight or flight" response . The response is instinctive: what provokes it is to some extent learned.

Cats' attachments to each other and to us are real and can be deep. If separated by distance or by death, cats can pine in ways that we all recognize.

HAPPY CATS, SAD CATS, AND CLOWNING CATS

The constant smile on some cat's faces is no more than an accident of anatomy; it's an emotion we think we see in the shape of the cat's muzzle. So is the constant scowl on the faces of some Persians. On the other hand, all of us who know our cats know the difference between "happy face" and "sad face". Some of our cats are happy more often than they're sad, and these are the cats we're more likely to think of as clowns with a sense of humour. It's our interpretation of cat behaviour that imbues some of their activities with humour. Some people tell me their cats have a sense of humour because their cats wait in ambush then unexpectedly leap on their ankles. That's play activity. Others tell me how their cats behave like clowns when they're hungry but that's really a conditioned response, the result of the activity being effective previously. Cat activity can certainly be funny. It can make us laugh and feel good. Some cats always look on the bright side of life, but personally, I have a little difficulty calling that a real sense of humour.

the ready-to-mate female dragging herself across the ground, moaning, with her bum raised in eager anticipation.

Most of us live with neutered cats, so we don't routinely see lustful behaviour, although a cat's response to catnip – rolling on the ground and acting weird – is similar to a cat's behaviour in response to a feeling of desire or lust.

Sadness or depression

Sadness is an uncomfortable feeling that I see in some cats when they have been separated from their home environment, for example when they are hospitalized. The sad hospitalized cat doesn't show any particular fear, anger, or worry, but it doesn't eat as usual, and it doesn't respond to play activity from the nurses. Once the cat returns home, its sadness

dissipates, and its appetite and activity levels immediately return to normal.

Depression is a rare and severe form of unhappiness, so severe that it overwhelms a cat's most basic survival instincts. The clinically depressed cat withdraws completely. It doesn't even eat or drink, seemingly losing the will to live. I have seen clinically depressed cats overcome their depression when they were reunited with their owners.

Disgust

If you have ever offered your cat less than perfectly fresh food, you will probably have witnessed feline disgust. A cat's liver is not capable of processing and eliminating many of the natural toxins that are produced in decomposing food. Their feeling of disgust in the presence of

naturally decomposing food is a wonderful survival behaviour.

Unfortunately the sense of disgust can be overwhelmed by a feeling of pleasure at something else, which is why cats will consume something that is dangerous and would normally be disgusting. For example, a cat that loves to drink running water may consume antifreeze, if this is added to the water in a garden fountain in winter to prevent it from freezing.

Training is logical

You may have noticed that your cat has worked out cause and effect and trots or even runs to the kitchen to the noise of its food container being opened. It has trained itself. Let me repeat a fundamental fact here: a cat's a cat, not a dog that purrs! While dogs may respond to verbal discipline, confident cats respond wonderfully only to rewards, primarily food but also toys or access to pleasure. Cats with little confidence are extremely difficult either to obedience train or train to play games.

Getting started

As with our kids, the very young are most open to learning. Adult cats can certainly be trained, but it takes a little more understanding of all those feelings and emotions I outlined on the previous pages. Older cats also usually need to *unlearn* doing what they're already doing before learning what you want to teach them. Start training as soon as your new cat joins your household. Train in a small, quiet room, just before mealtimes or just after awakening, and without other animals present. Keep the training sessions short, no more than two or three minutes per session.

Cats are different from dogs, but some of the best training practices apply to both. Rewards of food or toys and attention are powerful motivators.

An unexpected spritz of water can really discourage bad behaviour. "Soaker" water pistols with a longer range mean you can stand even further away, and your cat is less likely to notice that you are the source of the shock.

Motivators

Most kittens are motivated by food rewards, but with older cats it can be a challenge to find out exactly what's powerful enough to drive it to perform. Freeze-dried liver treats are a good starting point, and there are various commercial food treats to try. Whatever you use, don't be excessive with the rewards. If you're using your cat's regular kibbles, remember to include these when measuring its daily rations. It sounds harsh, but if treats don't motivate your cat, skip its meals for a day. A healthy cat will come to no harm if it goes without food for 24 to 48 hours, as long as it drinks. When food doesn't do the trick, find the type of toy that tickles its interest. Soft furries do it for some, while catnip toys do it for others.

Punishment and divine intervention

Punishment is pointless in cat training. Giving a cat a shake if you catch it chewing on your houseplants or jumping up on the kitchen work surface may satisfy your need to vent your anger, but all it will do to your cat is make it worry more about what you plan to do when you touch it. So will shrieking and screaming at it. The more you use punishment, the more likely your cat is to simply view you as a weirdo and avoid your touch, even your presence.

"Divine intervention" is different. This doesn't obviously come from you, but is a direct result of what the cat just did. For example, a cat jumps onto the kitchen work surface, lands on double-sided sticky tape, doesn't like the feel, and instantly jumps off. A cat jumps onto a bed, passes through an infra-red beam from a tiny burglar alarm that sets off a siren, doesn't like the sound, and escapes from the bedroom. A cat is about to scratch the sofa and – silently – gets a shot of water in its face from a water pistol.

All these are, from a cat's perspective, "acts of God", not punishment from you. Your aim in associating what your cat is doing with something mildly unpleasant is to train it in natural avoidance. All feral cats learn through experience how to avoid dangers. Be creative, but always take care to be kind with your use of divine intervention. Your aim is to train your cat to abandon whatever it wants to do because it's unexpectedly unpleasant, but never because it's painful.

BRUCE'S DISTRACTION TIP

I find a short, sharp hiss is a simple way to stop a cat in its tracks long enough for you to put it off what it's planning to do. Has your cat caught sight of a songbird in the grass? A sharp hiss, or any other similar noise, should distract it long enough for the bird to fly away or for you to get your cat. The hiss is part of a cat's natural verbal repertoire. Use this technique sparingly, however, otherwise your cat will learn that it means nothing.

If your cat sees its carrier as a bed or a hidey-hole every day, it is far less likely to put up a fight when being placed in it for a trip to the vet.

BRUCE'S REWARDS TIP

While dogs reliably respond well to food and then to verbal rewards, cats are different. It can be difficult to bribe a cat. Put some thought into exactly what your cat enjoys most: is it being stroked, being fed fresh prawns, chasing a feather on a string, or simply having a warm spot to lie in? Use access to the most potent reward in your cat's training.

A cat's logic is not your logic

You pick up the cat comb, and your cat vanishes. You get out the cat carrier, and your cat vanishes. You reach for an anti-flea aerosol, and your cat vanishes. Cats are always learning, and we can be very, very slow at noticing what's happening. If combing tangled hair hurt the last time, it's natural your cat will want to avoid that happening again. If your cat was frightened by a car trip and then a visit to some nasty stranger who stared close up at it, squidged its belly and felt its joints then, as often happens, stabbed it in the back with something sharp, it will want to avoid a repeat of that too. And if a strange cylinder was brought close and then hissed like the biggest, baddest cat ever, your cat will want to get away from that cylinder the next time it sees it.

Don't try reasoning with your cat. I haven't ever met a single cat that understands conditional sentences. Instead, try associating unpleasant objects with positives. Leave the cat carrier always open, with comfortable bedding inside it, perhaps even a few food treats. Groom your cat in different locations, not always the same place, and give potent rewards before, during, and after. Avoid flea sprays when you can; safe spot-on products are less threatening alternatives.

Nervous cats are challenging

Cats that were not humanized as kittens, "habituated" (to use the trainer's term) to interacting with us, find it difficult to differentiate between threatening situations and harmless activities.

These fearful cats find new experiences frightening. And its not just cats that didn't have lots of contact with us before they were seven weeks old, or cats raised by inexperienced mothers, that produce a new generation of nervous individuals. I've known cats that were born to competent mothers and raised in warm and caring human families that still mature into adults with nervous dispositions. Whatever the reason for

BRUCE'S TRAINING TIPS ON REALISTIC EXPECTATIONS

- Progress one step at a time and have clear goals for what you want your cat to achieve.
- If you're using a clicker, whenever possible have someone show you exactly how to pair the click to the reward. Timing is absolutely vital with clicker training.
- If you sense your cat is restless or not enjoying the session, stop and try again later.
- If your cat is fearful, don't even try training until its fear has reduced to a point where it is willing to eat with you right beside its food bowl.

CLICKER TRAINING

Clicker training involves using a small plastic clicker device that makes a clicking sound when you press it. That click sound acts as a "bridge" between your command and the reward. The click sound becomes associated with your cat getting a reward, so it learns to enjoy hearing that sound. Clicker training speeds up learning as long as your timing is perfect. Give a food reward and as it is taken, click the clicker. Soon the sound is almost as important as the reward. An alternative I used with my cat was to say her name when she took a treat. Soon, all I had to do was say her name and I had her attention. Timing is absolutely critical. Get one-to-one help for an hour or so from an experienced clicker trainer or watch a good demonstration on the internet, such as those by Karen Pryor, one of the founders of clicker training.

Clickers are simple and inexpensive. If you use them, it's worth buying a few so that you always have one to hand around the house or in your pocket.

their nervousness, these sweet, worried individuals spend their lives avoiding challenges. To them, your attempts to train them are another challenge.

Training takes great patience

When presented with a new challenge, the introverted, or nervous or fearful cat will do one of two things. It either hunkers down, sits motionless, and as it were buries its head in the sand. It is pretending that nothing is happening and hoping if it doesn't move, the challenge – you asking it to do something – will go away. Alternatively, it darts away and hides. Most cat owners I know find this distressing, and many respond as we

would if our kids behaved this way, with cuddles and reassurance. Unfortunately, that rarely works. Don't do it.

An anxious cat wants to be left alone, crouched in its corner or under whatever furniture it has found. Leave it there. Put a few of its favourite food treats nearby and leave the room. Your continued presence will only be seen as a continuing challenge, especially if you look directly at the fearful cat. Forget about any type of training until your nervous cat is relaxed enough to allow you to be in the same room while it eats, then closer to the food bowl and, if you're really lucky, beside it while it eats (*see* pages 120–1).

You cannot train a frightened cat. The first thing it has to learn is how to calm itself, and then how to stay relaxed and happy in your presence.

Basic training

Coming to you when called is the basic command, at the root of everything else you actively teach your cat to do. I'm calling this a command because that's the word typically used in dog training, but with cats we are in reality issuing requests. In a typical cat household, coming when called and speaking when asked is all we want from our cats. If they respond to these requests, we have enhanced both their safety and security and our own peace of mind.

All cats need training

Your cat doesn't just depend on you for food, shelter, and health care. Housebound cats in particular also depend on you for their education, for instructions in how to live enjoyably with us. Even though cats are "low-maintenance" pets compared with dogs, they still need basic training instructions. It's worth repeating: train when your cat is alert and hungry, for example just after it has awakened and before meals. Once you have successfully taught "Come" you might find that training is easier than you expected, and a whole lot more fun. If that's the case, I've also included ideas for a variety of other activities to train your cat to do. If you do these exercises, as well as your getting pleasure out of what you've achieved, your cat will have a productive outlet for the drive to think and do that all cats need to fulfil.

Start with target training

This is simple and fun. What you're doing is training your cat to follow a target – your hand or a short stick – in the same way it would follow more exciting things, like mice. You just show your cat a toy or a treat in your hand and when it touches its nose to it, you instantly praise with soft, friendly words (like "Good Milly") and give your cat the treat.

Once your cat understands that it has to touch its nose to the treat – and this is learned fast by some cats, much slower by others – continue to give immediate verbal praise to the nose touch, but start delaying the food or toy

Some people will tell you the way to a cat's heart is through its stomach, but in fact it's an excellent route to the brain.

reward. Soon, just your words of praise will be enough. I'd suggest you use two different types of targets: your extended hand and another item, such as a stick the length of a typical ruler, with a treat placed at the end.

BRUCE'S TIPS ON SOUNDS

Choose a sound signal to get your cat's attention – for example, calling your cat's name, giving a hand clap, or blowing a whistle, or perhaps a combination of your cat's name and another signal. Don't rely on a signalling device such as a bell or a shaken pot of vitamin tablets alone; you may not always have the sound-maker at hand. Use a signal you can always make wherever you are, indoors or outdoors. A sound maker is fine as a secondary signal, something that reinforces your words, clap, or whistle. For example, I called my cat Milly by her name, and combined that with making a shaking sound with the pot of vitamin tablets she craved. That means that at night, when I want her in, I don't have to shout her name and disturb my neighbours but just shake the vitamin container.

When using your hand as the target, present the food treat with your fingers below it and your thumb above. Really excitable cats might bite your fingers if the food treat is too tempting, so take care. If you think there's a risk, use the stick with the food treat on the tip.

Coming to you

Once your cat shows consistent interest in a treat, either in your hand or on a target stick, you can start active training. Show your cat the treat and praise it for paying attention to it. As it touches its nose to the target, move your hand towards you and say "Milly come". As your cat comes towards you, say "Good come" and as it reaches you give the reward. If you're using a clicker (*see* page 99), click when your cat first noses the treat and then again when it reaches your hand and is given its reward. It doesn't take much time for your cat to associate the word "come" or the click with moving forward and getting a food treat.

If your cat always comes when called, reward it less frequently. Intermittent rewards are better for reliable training than rewards given consistently. If your cat is less interested in responding to your command, start by rewarding it every single time until it comes consistently, then change to rewarding less often.

At first have your cat come only a very short distance, say 10cm (4in), but gradually increase this. Back yourself up each time you increase the distance. Your cat will see what you're doing and take it as a visual clue to what it should do. After a few sessions your cat will come from across the room when called. Given several short training sessions a day, within less than a week it should come from another room or anywhere in the house that it can hear its name and your request to "come".

TRAIN YOUR CAT TO ACT AS A MESSENGER

Extravert cats love interactive activities. Once your cat reliably comes when called, have both owners go to opposite ends of the room. One (let's start with me) calls the cat and gives a reward for compliance. I then say "Find Julia" and instantly Julia says "Milly come" and rewards Milly when she complies. Julia then says "Find Bruce" and as she finishes speaking I say "Milly come" and reward Milly when she does so with a "Good come". Milly learns that each time she's instructed to go to a particular person, that person calls her. In other words, she learns that person's name. Once she responds consistently and reliably within a room, she can be trained to come to each other from one room to another. And once that's done, if she's told to "Find Julia" she'll search until she does. If she does this you can attach messages like "Suppertime!" to her collar.

Coming to you

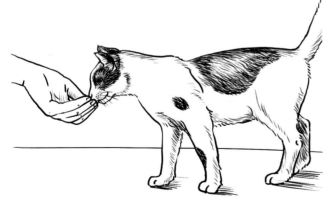

1 Once your cat is accustomed to touching a treat to get it, start slowly moving the treat away once it is touched, and say "Come" as you do so. Almost any cat will naturally follow the treat.

2 Don't be too ambitious – keep the distance short at first. A couple of steps is a good start. Then give the treat and say "Good come". Build up the distance gradually.

Sit

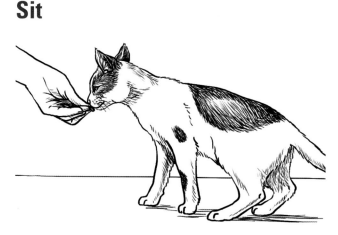

1 Start as with the other training, holding the treat on your fingers (or a target stick) and getting your cat interested in it. Always start with the treat about at your cat's natural nose level.

2 Move the treat up smoothly (don't snatch) not suddenly, or your cat will stop following it. As the head goes up and the rump down, say "Sit". Give the treat as soon as your cat is sitting.

Speaking when spoken to

Indoor cats not familiar with the outdoors are likely to be frightened and hide if they wander outside. Others do things they will regret: some climb trees and then once up in the branches become scaredy cats unwilling to climb down. Yet others will find themselves in places like cellars that they can't get out of. It's much easier to find a lost or hiding cat if it has been trained to miaow back when it hears its name called. If your cat is a natural talker, this training is quite easy, because you're simply channelling a natural behaviour. Training is much harder if your cat is not naturally verbal.

Have treats handy and when your cat speaks without your asking it to, say "Milly speak". As it does so give the treat. Evolve this to intermittent rewards, and within a few days your cat will "speak" when it hears your command to speak. Take care if your cat is already loquacious. If it's a constant talker (a typical Siamese trait) and that gets on your nerves, either don't train it to speak or do so because you want to then train it to be quiet. Remember, any behaviour you reward, including miaowing, will increase if that behaviour is rewarded.

Once you've trained your cat to speak on command, you may want to train it to be quiet. Do this by requesting "Milly speak" to your already trained talkative cat but don't give any reward. Instead redirect its attention to something else such as a thrown toy. When your cat interacts with the diversion, give verbal or food treat praise.

More basic training

Once you realize how easy it is to train your cat to come on your request and to speak when you ask it to do so, further cat training can become an unexpectedly delightful experience for both of you.

TREE-CLIMBING CATS

If your cat is up a tree and seems to be stuck, keep your cool. Most will eventually come down on their own. On the other hand, if someone the cat doesn't know puts a ladder up and tries to grab it, it is likely to climb even higher. Give tree-climbing cats some thinking time. Don't rush them. When you know the cat is hungry, ask it to "come" down, using its favourite food treats.

BRUCE'S LESSON-TIME TIP

Use distinctive words like "school time" when training begins and "finished" when it ends to let your cat know it's in a training session. Cats will quickly learn that these distinctive words mean "pay attention and you get treats" and "no more treats". Remember, timing is critical with rewards. Give praise and rewards at the same instant your cat complies with commands, not before or after.

Stay

1 Have your cat sit, but rather than immediately giving the expected treat say "Stay", then give the treat. Hold out another treat, repeat "Stay" and wait a couple of seconds before giving the treat.

2 Gradually extend the length of the 'stay'. As with all training, once your cat is responding reliably, you can move to giving intermittent treats rather than rewarding it every time.

Sit when asked

Hold the food treat in your hand at nose level and lift it up and back over your cat's head. As its head goes back to keep its nose in line with your hand, it will naturally sit. As it does so, say "Sit" and give the food treat as soon as your cat sits. If your cat stands on its hind legs to reach your hand, you're holding the treat too high. Just skim your hand a couple of centimetres (an inch) over your cat's head. If your cat backs up to keep its nose near your hand, do this training in the corner of a room where it can't back up.

Stay

"Stay" training naturally follows once "sit" or "lie down" training is reliable. You can start it straight from a "sit". Instead of immediately rewarding a "sit", say "Stay" and give the reward. Put another treat in your hand in front of your cat's nose, say "Stay" again, but now wait two seconds before giving the treat.

Gradually increase the interval between the request and the reward, seconds at a time. If your cat doesn't stay, go back to a "sit": when it complies, end the training session and try again when it's more in the mood. Eventually you should be able to get your cat to stay sitting or lying down for more than a minute.

Lie down

Start with your cat in a "sit" and let your cat nose the expected treat, but rather

YOUR CAT MIGHT NOT STAY

Cats find constant corrections annoying, so avoid frequently lifting and returning your cat to where you want it. Be patient. Go back a step when needed, or after a short "stay" ask your cat to "come" before it thinks about moving. Some cats learn to stay better on raised surfaces such as tables than they do on the floor.

than giving it, lower your hand (or stick target) to the ground between your cat's paws. As its nose follows the treat, slide your hand back towards you. Your cat will slide one foot forward, then the other; as it naturally drops to the floor, say "Lie down" and then give the reward.

Try this training in front of a bar that is too low for your cat to walk under, such as a brace across the legs of a chair. Let it

BRUCE'S TELLING-OFF TIP

A social reprimand such as saying "Bad girl" and avoiding eye contact with your pet for a minute works well with dogs, but it's pointless with cats. Dogs don't bear grudges but cats, in their own way, do. Threaten a cat with a nasty-sounding voice and it will remember that. Reprimand too frequently and not only will your cat not "learn its lesson" it is more likely to skip classes in future – or even pack its bags and leave altogether.

Lie

1 Start by bringing your cat into a "sit", with the treat held in front of its nose. Begin to bring the treat down and towards you, moving it slowly and smoothly.

2 As the cat follows the treat and slides its front paws along the floor, its shoulders inevitably sink. If there is a barrier in front of it about head height, it will sink even lower to slide under it.

3 As your cat's belly descends to the floor, say "Lie down" and reward it with the food treat. Once your cat will lie down reliably, you can ask it to "stay" in this position.

Roll over

1 When your cat lies down, the treat is in front of it. Move the treat forwards, not towards your cat's nose but down one side of its body. It will usually roll onto the other side to follow the treat.

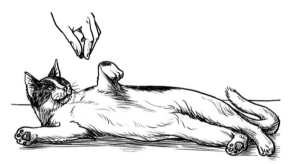

2 Keep moving the treat down towards the tail end and across the tummy, aiming for the uppermost hip. Your cat will raise its head and follow the treat with its eyes, nose, and maybe paws.

3 Sweep the treat over the body and your cat will roll. Say "Good roll over" and give the treat. If your cat just twists its shoulders, the treat was too far up the body: move it lower next time.

Jump

1 Start jump training without the jump: just tempt your cat to step from one chair to another following a treat.

2 Once the idea has sunk in, move the chairs apart. Say "Jump" as your cat jumps the gap.

3 As soon as your cat has landed, reward it with the treat. An extra treat here won't hurt either: you're not just rewarding your cat for the natural movements that result from following a treat, but for a positive action.

nose the food, then withdraw your hand under the bar of the chair, so your cat has to drop its head and its body to follow the treat. Once its head is under the bar let it nose the treat then give it.

Roll over

This is a good trick for relaxed, easy-going, Garfield-like cats that are happy to sleep on their backs or expose their undersides to their human family. It is more difficult for intense or hyperactive cats. Break this training into its component parts.

Starting from a "lie down" and a "down-stay", train your cat using food treats to lie on its side by moving the food treat down one side. Sometimes a little physical help from you is useful. When your cat is on its side, move the treat towards its upper hip, and as the eyes follow it, give praise and the reward. Once it does this consistently, make it rotate its body a little, following the treat, and reward with praise and treats. Next, move the treat over the body at the hips.

As it rolls over to keep track of it, say "Good roll-over" and instantly give the treat. Once your cat learns to roll over, you can give another request that it readily understands, such as "Sit", to get it out of the roll-over position, rewarding with a "Good sit" and an instant treat.

Some cats can be trained to roll over just for a belly scratch, but a food lure is a guarantee for the foodie cat.

BRUCE'S TIMING TIP

Say "Roll over", or "Die for your country", or whatever you want but let me repeat, ensure that the timing of your words is exact – when your cat starts to roll over.

Jump

Cats love climbing and jumping, so this is easy for your cat to learn and impressive when showing off to friends.

Place two chairs with nonslip surfaces about 25cm (10in) apart and put your cat on one of the chairs. Show the treat, then withdraw your hand until it is over the other chair. Your cat will follow (walking) and when it noses the treat, give the reward. Repeat this with the chairs a bit further apart until they are sufficiently separated to need a jump. As your cat jumps, say "Milly jump" then instantly give the reward in your hand and maybe one more. If you want to turn this into circus training, add a hoop!

Walking on a harness

Judging by what people tell me when they bring their indoor cats to the clinic, it's pretty much normal for owners to feel guilty about not letting their felines outdoors, but your guilt trip is unwarranted. Many cats are perfectly comfortable leading an indoor life; but if you want to give your cat the option of going outdoors, and its too dangerous for it to do so on its own, training it to walk on a lead is an option for any relaxed cat that's not fearful of the outdoors.

Choose a comfortable harness

You can use any type of harness. There isn't a "best" design: the best harness is simply the most comfortable one that is also escape proof. I like the flat type with a strap around the front of the chest attaching at right angles to a single or double strap around the body behind the front legs. A simple alternative is a corded figure-of-eight, with one loop of the eight around one forelimb and the other loop around the other. The lead attaches over the back where the two circles meet, and a cylinder lock slides down to tighten the harness snugly over the back. You should be able to fit a single finger anywhere under the harness. Too tight and it's uncomfortable; looser and your cat may be able to wriggle out of it.

Whatever harness you choose, accustom your cat to wearing it around the house. Put it on just before a meal, let your cat eat its food, then take the harness off. Little by little extend the lengths of time it wears the harness until it accepts it just as it accepts its collar. At this stage attach a short, lightweight nylon lead to the harness and let your cat drag it

A cat wearing a harness is an unusual sight, but need not be if it is trained from kittenhood to enjoy the feeling and taken to areas where it is not frightened.

around: make sure it doesn't get caught under furniture. And if your cat decides it's a great chase toy, simply move on immediately to the next stage, which is walking on the lead.

Walking itself on the lead

Start lead training indoors, with no distractions. An empty hallway is always a good place to begin. With the lead dragging behind, move in front of your cat and request it to "Milly come". As it gets to you say "Good come" and simultaneously give a succulent treat.

If your objective is simply to take your cat outdoors and let it walk where it wants to walk, with you guaranteeing its safety by holding onto the lead, move immediately to the final stage. Just take hold of the lead and let your cat do the walking, rewarding any movement with a food treat. Once your cat handles any tension it feels on the lead without resenting it, go outdoors to an area where it feels secure and, day by day, spend increasing amounts of time outdoors.

Walking your cat on its lead

If you want your cat to actually walk with you – to "walk to heel" in dog terms, you need to do a little more.

Once it is happy to come to you while wearing its harness and lead, call your cat to come, then sit, and reward each event. With your cat beside you, hold a food treat outside your leg where your cat is. It doesn't matter which side your cat is on or which hand you use.

Move forward with that leg and at the same time say "Milly walk" drawing your cat forward with the food treat. When your cat takes a step forward, give the reward, saying "Good walk". Gradually increase the number of steps it takes before it is rewarded. Once your cat gets the hang of it and walks forward beside you, give a "sit" request when you stop. Multiple instructions keep your cat's mind from wandering.

Walking on a harness is a comfortable compromise for those who feel the outdoors is not a safe place for their cat to roam, but don't want to restrict it to a life spent entirely indoors.

BRUCE'S LEAD-TRAINING TIPS

- Training to walk on a lead takes patience and it's only for confident cats who are not frightened of the outdoors.
- Don't start walking your indoor cat outdoors unless you plan to continue to do so. Exposure to the thrills of being outdoors followed by indoor confinement is unfair to your cat.
- Never apply tension to the lead. It's not for directing your cat to go where you want it to go, it's worn only for safety.
- Avoid parks with dogs or noisy, frightening places. A quiet, preferably fenced area is best.
- Don't let your cat get bored during a training session. If it pulls on its lead, wanting to go somewhere, go with the flow, don't pull back as your instincts might instruct. All that your pulling will do is convert your cat into an immobile silk brick.
- If you don't want to go where your cat is taking you, instead of pulling back, just pick your cat up, move elsewhere and start lead walking again.

For your cat, walking on a lead outdoors is a totally different experience from doing so indoors. The distractions and potential worries are so great that your cat will probably not at first be interested in food rewards or your training plans. Stay relaxed. Let your cat get accustomed to the sights, sounds and smells of where it finds itself. Work on the assumption that it will take many visits outdoors before you can start actual lead training in that new environment. And remember, your cat is never going to do anything to please you, as dogs do. Whatever it does, it does to please itself, either because it's simply enjoyable or because it knows you will give it a cool reward. Make sure that training, whatever it is, is fun for your cat.

Remedial training

Many, if not most, of us don't ever actively train our cats. We simply take feline good behaviour – using the litter tray, not biting us, accepting our petting and affection – for granted. That's why we think of cats as "low maintenance". Then, when the cat does do something that we don't want it to – scratches the furniture, urinates by the front door, grabs a passing ankle – it gets reprimanded, even punished. We don't realize it, but we're unwittingly using punishment-based training on our cats, rather than actively using a reward-based approach of "positive reinforcement". Is there any surprise, then, that it seldom works?

Get into your cat's mind

You cat may be sparky and bright-eyed, but it's not Einstein. If you discipline your cat when it does something you don't want it to, it simply associates the punishment with *you*, not with what you consider its misdemeanour. Not only does your attempt at training fail, your cat starts to fear you. It continues with its activities but now it darts away after doing what it's doing as fast as it can so you can't catch it! Just as commonly, it reserves its unpleasant activities for when

you're not there. If you think your cat is getting even with you, you're wrong! Unwittingly, you have simply trained it to do whatever it's doing in your absence.

Try to see what's happening from your cat's point of view. Whatever it's doing, from urine marking or scratching furniture to biting you when you pet it, is completely normal cat behaviour, but it's a behaviour we don't like. I didn't like it when Milly started batting my face at five in the morning, but cats are nocturnal, mentally and physically active and alert

just before dawn, and she wanted me to be active too, getting her breakfast.

Cats occasionally need to release pent-up energy. They need an outlet for their natural hunting activity, their impulse to stalk and attack. They need their mad moments when they release their steam valves. Your role is not to eliminate these activities; you can't. Retraining involves

Scratching is necessary, and using the most prominent thing in the room is unfortunately natural. It's up to you to provide an alternative that's attractive enough.

channelling these activities, so that your cat understands when, where, and with what it can do what it wants to do.

Most problem behaviours fall into a few simple categories: peeing or pooping in what you consider the wrong place; aggression towards people, other pets, or other cats; destructive activities or going where you don't want your cat to go. Problem behaviours increase in almost direct proportion to how many

cats share your home. Retraining almost always involves a combination of "divine intervention" (*see* page 97) when your cat does something you don't want it to, together with some basic positive reinforcement, in the form of reward-based training for doing what you want it to do – for example grooming its nails by scratching the place you have actively chosen for that activity.

Is the problem medical?

If your cat behaves in any way other than normal (for example urinates outside the litter tray or bites you unexpectedly when you pick it up), don't simply assume there is a behavioural problem. It could be medical. A cat with a bladder infection can associate pain when urinating with the litter tray itself and stop using it.

Cats' rarely soil their homes without some concrete reason. It may be physical, it may be psychological, but finding it is the key to stopping the behaviour.

A cat with an arthritic joint may bite when picked up simply because it hurts. Always check with your vet to make sure that a change of behaviour hasn't been triggered by a medical problem. Once you have the all-clear, you can concentrate on the behaviour side of the problem. Once you understand the reason for the behaviour, you can retrain your cat to behave the way you want it to.

Inappropriate elimination

The last thing a cat wants to do is soil its own home. That's why cats are pre-wired to dig holes in soil or sand, pee or poop in them, then rake over the material

Some cats urinate more frequently, often in strange places such as bathtubs, sinks, or even frying pans, because of a form of cystitis that is related to neurotransmitter chemicals in the brain. This cause of urinating outside the litter tray is surprisingly common, and may develop in any cat, but it is more common in indoor cats. Like other urinary problems, it needs medical and dietary management.

to cover the excavation. The smell of the used site brings them back to use it again and again. Cats arrive in our homes programmed to use litter trays, to behave as we desire animals living in the close confines of our homes should.

To maintain a cat's inherently hygienic toileting habits, all you need do is clean out its latrine every one to two days. That frequency depends on the type of litter tray you use and your cat's need for a hygienic tray. But it's not always that easy.

The most common reason cats are seen by cat behaviourists is "inappropriate elimination" – emptying the bladder or bowels where you don't want them emptied. In reality, while the cat's behaviour may be "inappropriate" to us, it's really doing what it's doing for logical and sensible reasons.

Unwilling to use a litter tray

Cats naturally dump on surfaces they can scratch and excavate, and learn from their mothers not just how to use a litter tray but also their excavation techniques in the litter. Mechanical-engineer mothers produce mechanical-engineer kittens, individuals that energetically dig and cover their pee and poop. Sometimes (and fortunately it's rare), kittens don't

learn from their mothers and don't arrive already litter trained. For unknown reasons, this is more likely to happen with Persian kittens than with any other breed or with moggies. Using a training pen for a few weeks almost always teaches the untrained kitten to use cat litter as a toilet, rather than your carpets.

Stops using the litter tray

More commonly, a previously well-trained cat stops using its litter tray and chooses another location for its toilet: behind a sofa, or in another room, or beside the litter tray but not in it.

The most common reasons a cat stops both urinating and defecating in its litter tray are because the tray has been moved, or the type of litter has been changed, or there's no privacy. Some cats stop using the tray if it gets too dirty; curiously, others stop if you're too fastidious when cleaning it.

Cats hate their litter tray near their food. Moving the tray accidentally closer to food (as one of my clients did to make more room for a dog bed), can cause a cat to stop using its tray.

In my experience, changing the type of litter is a more common cause. The feel under foot and the smell of the litter are both powerful reasons cats use a specific litter. Changing either, especially from an unscented to a scented variety, can trigger the abrupt stop in using the tray.

What is needed in both these circumstances is a return to the former arrangements. I'll explain feline privacy and the need for several litter trays if you have two or more cats under multiple cat problems (*see* pages 127–31).

It is more likely that a cat stops either urinating or defecating in the tray, but not both. In these circumstances it's very

possible there is a medical explanation. The cat associates the pain or discomfort it feels when urinating (from sharp urinary crystals or a bladder or urethral infection) with the tray. It wants to use the tray but in trying to avoid the pain urinates beside it. Similarly, pain from impacted anal sacs or constipation can, in the cat's mind, become associated with the tray, so it defecates beside it.

Spraying urine

Spraying urine is completely different. A cat naturally marks its home territory with its urine. While males are more likely to back up against a wall, door, or leg of a table and spray urine on it, both sexes may do so, even after they're neutered. Spraying is a normal cat activity, but it can be triggered unexpectedly by stress, for example when your cat feels threatened by a new person or animal in its home, or even by your moving furniture from previous locations. Another cat on your cat's territory is a classic stress, but sometimes it can be extremely difficult to work out why your cat has started spraying or urine marking.

Finding the type of litter your cat likes best can be a trial and error process. As a general rule, cats prefer the feel of sand or soil under foot to any other texture, so start with litters that feel like that to your cat. Clumping litter is easiest to clean but it can catch on the hind-leg feathering of longhaired cats. Covered litter trays offer privacy, and some come with odour-absorbing filters in the tops. Eco-friendly washable and re-usable litter also works well with most cats.

Whatever the cause, an anti-stress cheek-pheromone spray (Feliway) can help. I prefer the plug-in form that automatically emits spray throughout the day; simply place it in the room with the litter tray, following the product instructions. (*See* also multi-cat households, pages 121–5).

Retrain using an indoor pen

A retraining pen is a restricted area just large enough for your cat's bedding at one end and litter at the other. A good size is approximately 75cm (30in) wide and deep, and 65cm (26in) high. Fold-up ones are available, and are also useful as roomy transport in your car.

In a retraining pen, your cat has only two options: to soil its bed or to use the litter you have provided. Because cats are inherently tidy and simply hate soiling their own nest, almost all cats will urinate and defecate on the litter when given this option. Follow these steps when using a retraining pen.

1. After your vet has eliminated medical reasons for not using the litter tray, place a retraining pen in a quiet location where your cat has privacy when using the litter but also has access to seeing normal household activity.

2. Cat urine retains a powerful odour, even when you can't smell it. Your cat will go back to where it has soiled and do so again, unless you clean all soiled areas with an enzyme-based product, such as biological detergent, followed by alcohol, such as methylated or surgical spirit. Avoid ammonia-based cleaners; their smell prompts your cat to pee again.

Some people find this simple and hygienic, others find it off-putting. It really is your choice, because almost any cat can do it; far fewer will learn to use flush levers.

3. If training your cat to use a specific style of litter tray or a certain type of litter, install the tray in such a way that your cat has to use the tray to avoid soiling its bedding.

4. Watch your cat in the pen. When you see it using the litter tray, give it praise and a reward.

5. Take your cat out of the retraining pen only when you can concentrate your attention on it, for meals or for play, then put it straight back in.

In almost all circumstances you will need to use a retraining pen for one to two weeks to overcome any problem of your cat urinating where you don't want it to urinate.

Mitigating circumstances for messing in the home

Remember, your cat is not messing in your home to get even for something: there's always a sensible feline reason. The mitigating circumstances for not using the litter tray include:

- Bladder inflammation and an urgent need to urinate
- Diarrhoea that means the cat can't make it to the litter tray

BRUCE'S PROGRESS TIP

Once your cat is reliably retrained using the retraining pen, release it into a single room, with the litter tray just outside the retraining pen. If your cat has previously messed in that room, leave a bowl with food in it right on the previously messed location, even though you have thoroughly cleaned it. That inhibits the desire to mess on that spot again. Once your cat is reliably using the litter tray, gradually move the tray to where you want it to be in the room. Then, one room at a time, let your cat resume living throughout your home.

- It's too scary to use the outside latrine and there's none indoors
- It's cold or wet outside and there's no indoor litter tray
- The garden has been redesigned and the outdoor latrine is now a deck
- No privacy – the new pup stares!
- The tray was a suitable size for kitten but is too small for an adult cat
- A new litter doesn't feel or smell right
- The tray is beside something suddenly noisy like a washing machine
- The tray is next to the food bowls
- The tray is not clean or super-cleaned leaving unpleasant smell
- The cat is old and doesn't really care any longer

Train your cat to use your toilet

Personally, I prefer my cat to use her own toilet and my human family to use theirs, but if you really want to share yours with your cat, start by placing the cat's litter tray beside your toilet and place a similar toilet seat over the cat's litter tray. Over a few weeks, gradually increase the height of the litter tray using telephone books or other suitable articles, always rewarding your cat for using the ever-higher, toilet-seat-covered litter tray.

Once the litter tray and your toilet are the same height, your cat may naturally cross over and use yours. If not, purchase a tray that fits under your toilet seat, specially made to train cats to use human toilets. This allows you to put litter in the tray so your cat can cover its poop. Check out the internet for videos (search for cat toilet training kits) to see how they work. Flushing is best left to you, although if you're very committed to the idea, you might be willing to invest in the type of infra-red-beam automatic flush used in many public lavatories.

A certain level of aggression is normal feline behaviour: animals that evolved to pounce on prey for a living don't stop just because their food now arrives in a bowl.

as alternatives, your cat may use you as the only moving thing to attack. Play aggression – sudden aggression while playing with you – can arise from the same roots as predatory aggression.

Territorial aggression develops when a cat defends its territory from other cat competition, either within a multi-cat home (*see* pages 127–31) or against neighbour or feral cats outside your home.

And finally, cats may behave aggressively with you or other people because they are either tough, dominant and assertive cats or the exact opposite, fearful, apprehensive individuals. Pain, for example from injuries or illness, may also trigger aggression.

Love bites

This is surprisingly common, and is called "petting aggression" by behaviourists. You cat is relaxed and comfortable, beside you or on your lap, enjoying your stroking then *wham!* It bites you.

You may think the bite has come from nowhere, but it hasn't; your cat was probably giving you signals that it has had enough of all that touching. Stroking triggers mixed emotions. Cats like touch, because it's a distant memory of their mother's licking, but they are also worried by it, because adult cats don't make physical contact with others except when fighting or mating.

Some cats just get up and leave when they're fed up with your stroking. But when emotionally confused, a cat will typically flick its tail, turn and look at your hand, even flatten its ears back. Watch for these warning signals: if you

Cats are naturally aggressive

A pet cat may behave aggressively with you or the family dog, with other cats, or with potential prey such as birds, small mammals, and reptiles. Coping with an aggressive cat can be daunting. By "coping" I mean both channelling its aggressive desires and training it to inhibit its natural aggression, and success in either depends on understanding both

the cause and the type of aggression that a cat is exhibiting. As always, prevention is easier, cheaper, and faster than trying to overcome an aggression problem once it has developed.

Different types of aggression

Cats stalk, hunt, and kill; that's predatory aggression. If there is no natural prey to leap on, and if you don't offer toys ignore what it's telling you, you're leaving yourself open for a bite. If your cat does bite you, be theatrical. Shriek "Ouch!" even if it didn't hurt much. Your cat will associate your shrieking with its biting, and that mild diversion usually makes it stop and not want the same experience again. It will still come for contact comfort. By all means, stroke your cat, but let it initiate physical contact and avoid petting its belly, unless it asks for a belly rub. Watch its body language: if its whiskers rotate forward, stop immediately.

Predatory aggression

Cats are hard-wired to hunt for the thrill of the hunt. If your cat lives indoors and your home isn't over-run by rodents, then you (and your dog if you have one) are

---

BENGALS CAN BE FEISTY

I see lots of Bengal cats where I practice. They're exquisitely beautiful. They're also the cats most likely to show play aggression as kittens and dominant, assertive aggression with their owners.

Bengals and other recent hybrid breeds are naturally closer to wild cats than ordinary moggies – and closer to a cat that never domesticated itself.

---

the only prey available. Attacking ankles or arms is a natural activity, although sometimes there's a sexual element to it, even in neutered cats. Male cats ambush ankles more than females do. This is sometimes called play aggression.

To avoid your cat pouncing on you and biting, make sure you have active playing sessions with toys a couple of times each day. Choose toys that avoid direct contact between you and your cat, and use them not only for using up surplus energy but also for practicing hunting skills.

I like feathers or soft toys on a string hanging from a wand; dangle one for your cat to play with. Alternatively, drag a toy in front of your cat to induce it to pounce. Wrap some wool around a ping pong ball and roll it across the floor. You're aiming for a prey-like, slightly unpredictable movement.

If your cat gets overexcited with pouncing games, stop the game with a firm "No!" and resume once your cat is a little more relaxed. If your instinct is to play with your cat as you would with your dog, don't! Rough-and-tumble is a giggle for most dogs but can lead to play aggression with cats, especially if you use your own hand as a tease.

Finally, anticipate problems. If your cat always ambushes you in the same place, go prepared. Take a favourite toy and toss it ahead of you so that it becomes your cat's target, not your ankles.

PREVENT AGGRESSION

There are simple ways to reduce the risks of various types of aggression.

- Have your cat neutered before six months of age. Sex hormone doesn't just produce very stinky urine, it also triggers territorial aggression in males, with subsequent cat fights, and the development of a more reclusive personality in females, resulting in them reducing the time they're willing to spend being handled.
- Socialize your cat as early as possible and expose it to the variety of stimuli it will encounter in its adult life.
- Supervise your cat with other animals and with small children. Keep them apart in your absence if necessary.
- Avoid traumatic experiences such as unexpected noises or unknown people trying to touch or hold your cat. Keep calm and carry on.
- Give your cat daily exercise to enhance its familiarity with its environment.
- Don't play games that encourage biting.

Preventing hunting

Cats are amongst the most refined of land predators. Their teeth are perfectly shaped to render rodents immobile with a single bite, slipping between neck bones and severing the spine. But that's not what most pet cats do, unfortunately. They capture then torture the prey, or bring it to you – mother – to show you how successful they are.

If you have a problem with damaged or dead birds and rodents brought to you at dawn, try the following.

- As an alternative to stalking outdoors, create indoor games that compensate, allowing your cat to stalk, catch, and bite suitable furry toys. (This will not make your cat a more effective hunter!)

- Confine your cat indoors at its most successful hunting time. This is usually between dusk and dawn, but if it is a daytime hunter of garden birds, keep it in between dawn and dusk.
- If your cat goes outdoors at will, install an ultrasonic device in your garden that keeps birds away, and remove any bird feeding tables.
- Attach two or more bells to your cat's collar. Most cats quickly learn how to keep a single bell from ringing.
- Add a movement-activated ultrasonic device to your cat's collar.

Dominant, assertive aggression

Most cats use nothing more than subtle body language – for example, the direct feline stare – to assert their feelings of dominance within the home. However, some short-tempered cats use physical violence on people to assert their position. My sister's cat learned to smack her face when she was asleep and her ankles when she was awake if he wanted food. Some cats go much farther, for example attacking the new boyfriend who has moved in.

First impressions are lasting, and if the attached person behaves in any way that the cat sees as submissive, the cat wins and a subsequent attack is inevitable. Stand your ground, although doing so can be genuinely scary. For the most dangerous villains, cat behaviourist Vicky Halls suggests full biker leathers and a full-face helmet! As a simpler alternative go armed with a soft cushion either to throw at the cat or to hold up for protection. And no kidding, wear heavy gloves. For cats that really hate water, a powerful water pistol may work.

Whatever you do, don't let the bruiser think that it won. That inevitably leads to more aggression.

Fear-triggered aggression

A frightened, fearful cat will use body language – hissing, spitting, hunkering down and baring all weapons – to avoid a physical confrontation. But if the perceived danger doesn't disappear, it will attack. We see this frequently at the clinic when feral cats are brought in for treatment or surgery.

Below *Fearful aggression, such as when a cat meets an unfamiliar dog, is a natural defensive reaction. If the pup keeps its distance – and most do, certainly if they've met a cat before – this will go no further.*

Right *Cats instinctively hunt and fend for themselves, even though you feed them. If you fight this behaviour, you will lose: channel it instead.*

If you must handle a fearful cat, avoid sudden movements and loud noises. If you can quietly manoeuvre it into a corner, do so and then throw a dark blanket over it. Wrap it thoroughly. It will feel more secure in its dark, quiet enclosure while it is moved. (For counter-conditioning a fearful cat see pages 120–1.)

Redirected aggression

This is also known as pain-induced aggression, and both names describe it well. A cat is brought to the clinic, I do something to it, perhaps just examine it and take its temperature, it goes home and punches up its feline buddy, or bites its owner. That's redirected aggression.

Or you step on your cat's tail. She shrieks and attacks not your foot, but your other cat who happens to be sitting nearby. That's redirected aggression.

This is more common than you may think, and whatever triggers it, it can be so rewarding for the attacking cat, with the release of excitement chemicals in the brain, that it is difficult to overcome. To do so, provide your attack cat with other sources of excitement. For example, if it's always indoors and you can provide safe outdoor access, do so. And needless to say, see your vet for treatment of all underlying medical conditions that could cause pain to your cat, triggering the attack behaviour.

BRUCE'S FORAGING TIP

An effective and practical way to divert a cat's energy away from exciting games – such as stalking ankles, biting hands, or leaping onto passing people from great heights – is to make them search for their food. Use the tastiest dry kibbles, such as a premium kitten food. Once you have discovered the tastiest, instead of giving it in the cat's food bowl, place small quantities in paper bags or cardboard boxes throughout your home. Put them in opened cupboards, behind furniture, and on top of wardrobes, and let your cat search for them. Be precise with your measuring so that you're offering exactly enough to keep your cat lean and healthy.

Fear can be learned

Not all fearful cats are born that way.
A cat can suddenly and inexplicably lose
its confidence. We want to make sense of
everything our cats do, but sometimes it's
impossible to discover what triggers a new
fearful behaviour. I'm sure it's a sequel
to an event that traumatized the cat,
but the event can be so inconsequential
in our eyes that we miss it. A common
consequence is an "agoraphobic" cat, an
individual that feel safe in one room but
tense and vigilant outside of it.

This is different from the inherently
shy cat that is timid from kittenhood;
the inherently fearful cat is not one that
responds well to training, but cats that
have learned their fear can also learn to
overcome it.

Train to reduce acquired fear

Increase your cat's confidence, first in
its safe room by keeping it company,

> #### BRUCE'S FEARFUL CAT TIP
>
> Your natural instinct may be to pet and
> cuddle your fearful cat. That reassures
> dogs, but human touch may make an
> anxious cat even more fearful. It's better to
> let the cat find a safe hiding place and to
> leave it alone.

talking to it, feeding it, and giving some
comforting strokes outside of its safe
corner, cupboard, or other hiding place.
Once it is comfortable anywhere in the
room, expose it to wider areas, using the
same rewards of your companionship,
affection, and food. Expand the range
room by room, but first carefully inspect
each room for new or novel items that
might provoke fear. Cats can be spooked
by almost anything – as I learned in one
instance, even by a gym kit bag left
where it hadn't been left before.

I'd also use a cheek-pheromone spray
(Feliway). It's relatively cheap, will
certainly do no harm, and may be
beneficial. If the fearful, agoraphobic
reaction is intense, discuss with your
vet using an anti-anxiety drug such as
clomipramine. Take care with diazepam
(for example, Valium) and related drugs.
Some cats are known to have adverse
reactions to these drugs.

If your cat is anxious, follow these basic
guidelines day-to-day:

- Let it find its own hiding places where
  it feels safe, and don't disturb it there.
- Never force your cat to confront
  what frightens it. For example, if it is
  frightened of a particular area, such as
  where the washing machine is, rather
  than take it there to show it there's
  nothing to be frightened about, induce
  it ever so slowly closer to the room
  until it enters of its own free will.
- Avoid direct eye contact. That's scary
  for shy cats.
- Avoid stroking and petting. Use
  gentle words, games, and food treats as
  rewards and enticements instead.
- If your scaredy-cat loves a particular
  food, try offering it from your extended
  hand, always crouching down very low
  and looking away.
- Encourage prey-hunting play. This
  is a deep-rooted instinctive feline
  need. Dangling a small soft toy on
  a fishing rod can trigger interest in
  even the most nervous cat, and its fear
  temporarily diminishes.
- Stick to routines. Most cats dislike
  changes, and shy cats hate them.

*Never try to haul out a cat that has "gone to ground"
under furniture or coverings. Leave it alone, or tempt it
out with treats or a toy dragged on a string.*

If you live with a scaredy cat, provide bolt-holes around the home for when visitors call. If there's no sofa to hide under, a pet carrier or even cardboard box will do.

- Avoid changes to your cat's living space. Even moving furniture around can trigger worry and fear in a shy cat.

Timid cats benefit from calm care

Living with a timid cat can be frustrating, and the rewards are subtle. The return we treasure most from confident cats – physical contact with them – is there in only tiny amounts with fearful, shy, or timid cats. There is, however, another reward: the satisfaction that you're providing a scaredy-cat with a safe and secure home and by doing so, you are making its life so much better.

ANXIETY-REDUCING PRODUCTS

"Anti-anxiety" drugs for humans are only rarely licensed for use in cats. Drugs such as amitriptyline, fluoxetine, and clomipramine may be prescribed by a vet, but their side effects are even more unpredictable in cats than they are in us. Use them with caution.

Old fashioned anti-histamines such as diphenhydramine or hydroxyzine cause sedation as a side-effect. Although mostly used to treat allergic conditions, their relaxing effect is useful to manage some stressful situations. Non-drowsy anti-histamines such as cetirizine and loratidine are of no use for treating feline stress.

Feliway is a synthetic cheek-pheromone spray that has proved effective in double blind studies (where the dispensing vets and cat owners don't know what is in the product they are giving to cats). It is used to treat a variety of anxiety-rooted problems, such as urine marking in multi-cat homes or fear when staying at a cattery or being transported in a carrier to the vet.

Catnip, the mint-family plant containing nepetalactone as its active ingredient, triggers a euphoric response in some cats and by doing so diminishes stress. In rare circumstances it may trigger aggression. Catnip can be applied to scratching posts or used as stuffing in toys.

Alternative therapies such as homeopathic remedies and flower essences are marketed to reduce feline stress. As far as I'm concerned, if it's safe and it helps, use it.

It's vertical, it's wooden, it's in the middle of the room what could possibly be wrong with using such a perfectly designed scratching post?

BRUCE'S SCRATCHING POST TIP

Cats scratch to leave visible markers, which are obvious to any other cat that enters its territory. This is why sofas, often central in the room, are so perfect for scratching. Initially place a scratching post in a very visible location, such as just beside the arm of the sofa. Once your cat is routinely using the provided scratching post, you can move it daily, a little at a time, into a less prominent position. Ensure you provide an alternative scratching post at the one or two locations where your cat scratches. If it scratches at three or more sites, especially if you have two or more cats, consider stress as a possible complicating factor and consult your vet. More subtly than the visible marks, scratching also leaves scent from glands on the paws. Use an enzyme detergent to remove odour molecules from where your cat is scratching. Otherwise, it may return to its scent and scratch once more, even though you are providing an attractive alternative scratching post.

DECLAWING CATS IS A CULTURAL ISSUE

In some countries cats routinely have all their nails removed when they're neutered. In other countries this type of surgery is considered a mutilation, and performing it is enough to have a vet's licence to practice revoked. Personally, I performed this operation in the first years after I graduated, but I stopped once I thought about what I was doing. I haven't declawed a cat now for over 30 years. I think it's a barbaric procedure.

Cats are destructive

The third major problem we have with our cats is their natural need to scratch. All cats use the claws on their forepaws to scratch, not just upright objects but also at the earth, or our carpets, to rake as they do after using a litter tray. Of course, we consider this unacceptable damage to our property.

But cats are destructive in other ways too. Some scratch us, while others scratch and chew our clothing, especially our woollens. Indoor cats commonly eat houseplants, and any confident cat is likely to explore and cause damage where we don't want cats to go.

Scratching furniture

Scratching is as normal and necessary as eating, drinking, urinating, and defecating. It's hard-wired into your cat's brain. A cat simply must scratch, to exercise its claws, sharpen its nails, and stretch its muscles. Scratching has another vital role: visible scratches act as territory markers. They are also scent markers containing glandular secretions from the cat's paws.

Your cat simply has to scratch, so redirect this powerful need to a place that's acceptable to you. Ensure your cat has at least one and preferably two attractive objects such as scratching posts to scratch. Most cats like to scratch vertical objects like posts, but some like or even prefer scratching on a horizontal plane. These are the carpet scratchers! Learn what your cat likes, then provide a suitable alternative surface.

If your cat is obsessed with a piece of your furniture, cover the affected area with sticky tape, aluminium foil, or fine nylon netting. Fix the netting firmly over the area being scratched. Your cat's claws catch in the thin but tough nylon, and they don't like that. Take care with the size of the mesh: it must be fine enough to

SCRATCHING POST DESIGNS

Cats prefer rough surfaces like tree stumps to scratch, but if you use a natural tree trunk be prepared to vacuum up bits of bark at least daily. Ensure the post is tall enough for your cat to do full aerobic scratches; some are really only suitable for kittens. The post should be sturdy enough to not fall over when vigorously used. Take care with carpet-covered posts – some cats extrapolate and may start scratching your carpets too. For the same reason, if you have sisal carpets, make or buy a scratching post made from completely different material; otherwise, sisal is a good choice, because cats enjoy the feel of it. Finally, don't throw the post away when it looks disgustingly shredded. That's exactly how your cat wants it, and it's covered in fragrant paw scent.

Scratching also means stretching, so look for a post that is a little taller than your cat at full stretch. Some cats prefer surfaces at different angles.

Cats have to eat meat, but they also need their greens and they often appreciate them fresh.

ensure your cat can't catch its foot in it. If that happens, you're more than likely to end up with cat in hysterics!

At the same time, actively condition your cat to scratch the scratching post that you've provided. Leave food treats around the new post. If your cat is a catnip lover, rub catnip on it. Call it to "Come" to the scratching post, rewarding it for doing so. Your cat will soon think of the scratching post as something positive. Using a food lure, coax it to put its forepaws on the post, giving a reward as it does so with good words and the treat. Each time your cat repeats putting

its feet on the scratching post stretch out the time a little more before giving the reward. It won't take much time before your cat goes to the post for the added pleasure of having a good stretch and a nail manicure.

Eating houseplants

Cats naturally consume fibre from the carcasses of their prey. In the absence of this natural roughage, many if not most chew on various types of grass. Outdoor cats are quite selective about what they chew on. Indoor cats have less choice, and so are more likely to chew on whatever houseplants or cut flowers are available, including vegetation they would normally leave alone outdoors.

Provide safe grass for your cat to chew on; tubs of grass seed are readily available from pet shops and vets for this. At the same time, take an inventory of your houseplants and cut flowers and remove any that are poisonous, such as lilies (*see* pages 167).

Once you have safe alternatives in place, surround your existing houseplants with protection such as double-sided sticky tape or aluminium foil. I've found that set mousetraps covered with newspaper around the plant works; paw pressure on the newspaper springs the trap, and the sudden noise and the paper erupting in front of it scares the cat away, while the thickness of the paper prevents it from being injured.

DISCOURAGE DESTRUCTIVE BEHAVIOUR

Be theatrical but also imaginative in the ways you discourage destructive behaviour while preventing your cat from associating any mild unpleasantness with you. A powerful water pistol squirted on your cat as it approaches the arm of your sofa will be effective with many but not all cats. So will a sudden noise, for example an empty soda can filled with a few coins thrown on the floor. Clear, sticky strips available from pet shops are usually safe to apply to the arms and legs of scratched furniture. Your objective is for your cat to associate something mildly unpleasant with what it is just about to do.

Wool-sucking and people-sucking

Chewing or sucking on wool is a particularly Siamese-cat pastime, although related breeds are also more likely than average to chew on fabric. The fact that this destructive behaviour occurs more frequently in one breed than in others strongly suggests there is a genetic base for the problem. That, however, is academic: finding slobber on your woollies, or worse, neat holes in your cashmere, is downright irritating.

One theory is that suckling from mother provides a kitten not only with nourishment for six weeks but also with social and behavioural development for another six weeks. Kittens removed from their mothers before they complete that second six weeks of comfort suckling are more prone to wool sucking.

Wool sucking simply makes the sucker feel good: it releases dopamine in the brain, the same chemical released when an addict partakes of his addiction. That is why some cats don't restrict their sucking to wool, they suck us too, especially near smelly bits like armpits. Chewing on other strange items – washing up gloves, plastic bin liners – inexplicably does the same for other cats. The behaviour is technically called "pica" and although it is sometimes caused by a medical condition or diet deficiency it is also a quirky behaviour condition.

Wool-sucking is most likely to occur in mentally active cats that need something to do, so provide exciting activities that are likely to stimulate the brain to secrete dopamine. Prey games (see page 117) are effective. As another incentive, hide food around the house for your cat to find. Kibbles in paper bags are perfect but remember to deduct these from the regular meal. Something really tasty such as a chicken neck or lamb bone is a great diversion for most cats although potentially dangerous for individuals that, dog-like, bolt down their food.

If your cat is obsessed with chewing on something it shouldn't, offer something else more acceptable, then issue everyone in your home with noise-makers and water pistols and instructions to "shoot on sight" when your cat is about to misbehave. Adding a bell to its collar will let you always know where it is.

Demanding behaviour

Don't let your cat train you about what it eats: it lives in your home, not a feline restaurant. If your cat demands your attention at night, ignore it, and banish it from the bedroom. If it yowls outside the bedroom door, get earplugs. If you worry about the noise waking your neighbours, buy them boxes of chocolates and explain you're having a little trouble with a mobster cat but you'll win within a few days. You will, won't you?

Make sure your cat has other interesting activities rather than just interacting with you. The more it relies on you for play and excitement, the more demanding it will become.

Walking on tables and work surfaces

Confident cats love hanging out in high places, indoors as much as outdoors. The back of a sofa is fun, and the top of a wardrobe even more so, especially because heat rises and it's often warmer up there. A work surface or table offers an even more powerful reward: food – our food! Cats quickly learn that there's often butter or (even better) meat or eggs for the taking on your kitchen work surface or dining room table.

Cats enjoy looking out over their domain, and naturally enjoy heights,

Your cat might like to move in high places, but there are often good health-and-safety reasons to discourage this, at least in specific areas.

so provide them with appropriate high resting areas. One inventive client of mine built shelving steps onto the wall over his fireplace, allowing his cats to climb up to even larger shelves that were dressed with comfortable cat beds. A window bed is a simple and practical alternative to a wall of cats over your fireplace, or you can buy purpose built high resting areas – kitty condos – from well stocked pet shops or internet websites. Some reach to the ceiling.

Redirect your cat's need to hang out in a high place by training it to use a window bed or kitty condo. Use rewards and training in the same way you taught it to jump from one chair to another (*see* page 105).

Now that it has its very own elevated area where it can lie in the warmth and survey its territory, you can start training it to avoid jumping up onto tables and work surfaces. Needless to say, don't leave tasty food on your kitchen counter when you are not in the kitchen. If you find your cat on a table or work surface, or see that it's about to jump onto it, hiss! Spit that hiss! Sound cat-nasty, but follow through by coaxing your cat to the approved high area.

Training in your absence

Avoiding a problem is always easier than retraining. If you're going out and don't want your cat on the kitchen counter, don't let it in the kitchen while you're gone. If you have an open-plan home and that's not possible, creatively set "traps" for your cat. Position double sided sticky tape or aluminium foil so it will land on them when it jumps on the work surface, or pots and pans that crash to the floor if it tries to get on the surface; anything safe but unpleasant, so that your cat continues to learn in your absence through "divine intervention" (*see* page 97).

Above *Double-sided sticky strips or tape are unpleasant for a cat's paws, but not harmful. Leave them in place until your cat leaves the area alone and forgets about it.*

Left *To a cat, there's no obvious reason why a china shelf is off limits. You have to make and fix those boundaries in your cat's mind before a broken stack of cups does.*

Problems within the multi-cat household

Don't make the common mistake of thinking that two cats will automatically be company for each other: it's more likely they won't. More than one cat in a territory as small as a human household is stress-making for most cats. Cats look upon their homes as their "resources" their source of food, comfort, protection, warmth and security. Anything that threatens their resources causes stress.

Moving to a new home, a new baby in the family, the presence of strangers: all of these can trigger emotional conflict, but the greatest threat doesn't come from a new pup or from your moving your furniture around – it comes from the presence of another cat.

We're good at reading stress in other people's facial expressions, but cats appear inscrutable. They don't give much away in the look in their eyes. Instead, they convey their feelings through actions, including increased marking activity, scratching furniture, urinating outside the litter tray, leaving their faeces unburied or in new places, over-grooming, excessive vocalizing, eating too much, not eating, or even burning bladder inflammation.

Human siblings often fight as children then live together harmoniously when they grow up; with cats, it's more likely to be the other way around.

We think of these as behaviour problems, but it's more accurate to see them as cries for help. The best way to overcome these activities is to understand why they are happening, then whenever possible, to improve on the stressful circumstances. And distressing as it is for us, sometimes the only way to solve a problem, to make life better for the stressed cat, is to rehome it in a new home where it will be the only cat.

SIBLING RIVALRY

Getting two kittens from the same litter is an excellent choice and usually, after the first year of vigorously playing together and sleeping cuddled up as a single ball their relationship, although cooler, remains understanding and respectful. But not always. Brothers or sisters may hate living together and show their anxiety in typically feline ways, by urine spraying, wall- and furniture scratching, defecating outside the litter trays, or engaging in actual fights. In extreme instances, the only effective treatment is permanent separation.

Urine spraying

Spraying urine is just about the simplest way a cat can leave visual and smell messages for other cats. Sprayed urine is subtly different from squatted urine. It appears to be a bit more oily, and I've sometimes wondered whether any anal sac substance might also get mixed with it. Cats can certainly differentiate between sprayed and squatted urine, taking much more interest in the former.

In a multi-cat household, spraying is perhaps just the most obvious indicator of turbulent relationships. Don't be surprised if furniture is also scratched, to leave more visible and scented messages, or if all faeces isn't raked and buried in the litter as previously, or if poops are dumped outside the litter tray.

Reasons for spraying

Cats spray urine for two completely different reasons: either because of stress and a feeling of vulnerability, or the polar opposite, as an assertion of confident territorial ownership.

Sexually active cats spray to indicate readiness for mating, but spraying is not limited to intact cats. Neutered outdoor cats living in areas visited by other cats spray in prominent locations, such as on fences and bushes or on the trails of other cats. An outdoor cat may come through your cat's cat flap and spray indoors as a claim to your cat's territory, and even neutered indoor cats spray if a strange cat comes through the cat flap.

The frequency of indoor spraying is directly in proportion to the number of cats in the territory. One cat is unlikely to spray, two are more likely. If you have three cats, there is over a 50 per cent chance that your home will be treated to the pungent aroma of cat urine, and if you have as many as six cats it rises to over 80 per cent. If you have lots of cats, be prepared for liquid communication.

Bed-wetting and soiling

This is a real nasty, and speaking from my experience not at all uncommon in multi-cat homes. You get into your bed and find a wet patch – or even poop. This is probably the tip of the iceberg, an individual cat's ultimate sign of insecurity in the presence of other cats. Check out your home very carefully and you'll probably find scratch marks on doors or wallpaper and urine spray on table legs or stair banisters. Watch your cats' interactions. There are probably threats, even fights.

BRUCE'S BED-WETTING TIP

The other cause of wetting your bed, besides stress, is bladder or urethra pain caused by infection or inflammation. Always have your vet eliminate physical causes for bed wetting before concluding that the cause is behavioural.

A simple cat flap is fine where there are few cats. In more densely populated areas, collar-activated flaps are a better idea, and you may need to lock them completely at times, for example to keep out hooligan cats at night.

Cat flaps are a mixed blessing

A cat flap gives your indoor cat free access to the outdoors, but it also gives any confident outdoor cat free access to your home. I didn't know my neighbour's cat routinely visited our home until my neighbour told me his cat brought dead mice in traps to him each morning. We had a mouse plague and I just couldn't figure out what was happening to the traps I'd been setting!

Once a strange cat has come through your cat's cat flap, your resident is forever on the alert. "What's that noise?" "Who's there?" Even worse, it goes into the kitchen in the morning and there's a stranger, eating its food, using its litter tray, smoking its cigars. For some cats that's terrifying. For more confident ones it's a challenge that can't be disregarded.

If you have an "anyone can use it" cat flap, be prepared for the scent of sprayed urine. One survey found that over 50 per cent of homes with unlocked flaps had sprayed urine problems. Don't assume that a magnetic or microchip operated cat flap always solves the problem. They don't work well if your cat is racing back at speed. Also, some Atilla-the-Hun-type unneutered territorial toms find these cat flaps easy to break just by using brute strength. If your singleton cat is spraying because another cat is coming through the cat flap, or the stranger is spraying to claim your home as its territory, the only solution that works is to board over the indoor side of the flap, as a visual signal to your cat that the port of entry is permanently closed.

Left *Toileting places are personal – above all they smell personal to a cat. Provide plenty, and be prepared to place them well apart for privacy.*

Opposite *Outdoor access can make all the difference in a multi-cat household. It literally provides breathing space, giving the cats a larger territory to spread out in.*

Retrain a urine-marking cat

After reducing the stresses caused by the presence of other cats and modifying your home to accommodate those that live there, treat much as for all unwanted urinating (*see* page 115). Stop further urine marking by preventing the marker from having access to the sites where urine is left. After thoroughly cleaning and deodorizing any urine marks, spray synthetic cheek pheromone (*see* page 121) in all areas that have been scent marked. In some circumstances it may be necessary to use anti-anxiety medication, such as clomipramine, as prescribed by your veterinarian. Medicines such as these are not magic bullets. They don't work on their own, only in conjunction with reducing stresses and retraining. A training pen with bed, food, and litter tray may also be needed for a few weeks.

Deal with cat-to-cat aggression

Cats attack each other only as a last resort. Aggression is avoided through body language and voice but can quickly escalate from passive to active, and it's surprising how easy it is to miss the passive signs, to not realize that your sweet cats actually hate each other. Signs of passive aggression include:

- Direct stare from the dominant cat
- Sitting in a doorway or hall blocking passage to other cats
- Hissing or growling at each other

If your cat is responsible for organized crime in your neighbourhood, it's really up to you to be honest and to control the aggression. Train your cat to come in when called. Keep it in at night and provide indoor activities to satisfy the need for physical and mental stimulation. If it's attacking a specific neighbour's cat, talk to them. Offer to install a magnetic or microchip operated cat flap to replace their present one. Give them a water pistol and encourage them to use it if your cat visits their property. Attach bells to your cat's collar so they can hear the thug's approach. If a cat is coming on to your cat's territory, act as family backup. Shriek or scream at the intruder, squirt it with a water pistol. (When a feral cat threatened my cat in her own garden and I happened to have a glass of apple juice in my hand, I discovered that cats hate apple juice on them. That intruder never returned.) If it's coming through your cat's flap, board up the flap outside.

Territorial scratching

If a cat uses only one or two locations to scratch, it is just exercising its muscles and maintaining its pin-sharp claws. Dealing with this is simple: train your cat to use alternative scratching posts (*see* pages 122–4).

If, however, there are scratch marks throughout your home, especially around doors and windows and at entrances to hallways, these are there as visual and scent signals to other cats. They may be left either for your own cats or for others that come in through your cat's flap.

Excessive furniture- and wall-scratching is a sign of stress. The only effective treatment is for you to determine what is stressing your cat, then eliminate it. Keeping an outdoor cat from entering your home is simple. Investigating the politics within your multi-cat home is more complicated and may need the help of an experienced cat behaviourist or your veterinarian. The experienced behaviourist will notice subtleties that are easy to miss and give recommendations on what to do. Advice may include

using synthetic cheek-pheromone spray (*see* page 121) to reduce anxiety or using prescription anti-anxiety drugs. A vet experienced with using drugs can select which may be most useful. Not all veterinarians are familiar with the use of drugs as an adjunct – not a sole treatment – for problems in multi-cat homes.

How to maintain a peaceful multi-cat household

Most cats have, at best, a tenuous grasp of the concept of sharing. You can minimize the risks of living in a dysfunctional feline household in a number of ways.

- Keep a common-sense number of cats according to the size of your home, your garden, and the neighbourhood population. Don't hoard!
- When choosing littermates, get opposite sexes as there will be less sibling rivalry between them.

The Burmese believes its home is its castle – a trait shared to some extent by the closely related Tonkinese.

- Don't add another cat to a stable multi-cat home. If you must, choose one known to be sociable with others.
- Provide one litter tray for each cat you have, plus one more.
- Place a litter tray on each level of your home – remember to clean them *all*.
- Offer individual food and water bowls for each of your cats, not in a perfect row but scattered around the kitchen.

BURMESE HOLD THEIR OWN

It may be sensuous and beautiful, with a seductive sheen to its coat. It may feel like a heavy, warm, silk brick in your hands. It may be loving to you, but the cat most likely to pro-actively defend its territory is the Burmese. Cat behaviour people call them the thugs of the cat world, gentle and affectionate at home, despots outdoors.

MASKING ODOURS IS DIFFICULT

Lemon peel behind the television, polythene over the bed, pepper on the front door mat, pine cones in corners – forget about just masking urine odours or preventing further damage. All this will do is send your cat somewhere else to urinate unless you find out why it is happening. Determine the cause, and eliminate that. Until you can, restrict your cat to a pen where it can feel more secure.

- Feed several meals each day or provide dry food available for grazing on throughout the day.
- Provide many tall scratching posts.
- Provide a variety of both high and private resting places, and just as with litter trays, make sure there is at least one warm, comfortable location for each cat, plus one more.
- If there are no problems with outdoor cats coming in, give your cats routine access to your garden.

Chapter 4
Cats do what cats do

Maintain good health

Every cat inherits a starting potential for health and longevity within its genes. For example, many Siamese cats inherit the likelihood to live longer than other cats, while equal numbers of Persians inherit the prospect of shorter lives than average. Onto this potential we add the influences of living with us. Through the food we feed our cats, the environment we keep them in, and both the preventative and "fire engine" veterinary care we provide them with, we influence how healthy they are and how long they live. Maintaining good health starts with a safe environment, nourishing food, and control of infectious disease and parasites. Early neutering also reduces risk and prolongs life.

Create a healthy environment

The indoor-versus-outdoor debate has no conclusive answer, but there is no denying that outdoor cats live shorter lives than indoor ones, not just because of the greater risk of fatal injuries outdoors, but also because of the array of potentially lethal viruses that cats come in contact with when they meet and sometimes fight with cats that carry these viruses.

Infections from two of these viruses damage the immune system and predispose cats to the development of lymphoma, the most common feline tumour. Outdoor risks from transmissible diseases are dramatically reduced through sensible use of existing vaccines.

Vaccinate wisely

Preventing disease through inoculation, or vaccination, is a technique that harnesses the body's natural ability to fight infection. An infectious agent such as a virus or bacteria is modified so that it is no longer infectious, either by killing it, modifying it so it is still alive but no longer infectious, or taking vital components of it and enslaving bacteria through genetic engineering to produce replicas of these parts. The resulting vaccine is still similar enough to its unmodified form that when the immune system is exposed to it, the immune system creates antibodies, which are proteins that attach to and help destroy the specific infectious agent.

Kittens acquire some protective antibodies from the milk they suckle from their mothers soon after birth, but these temporary antibodies usually last around six to ten weeks. A variety of vaccines is available for cats, and some should be used in all cats, including the following.

Feline infectious enteritis

Also known as feline panleukopenia or feline parvovirus, this can survive for long periods in the environment. It causes severe vomiting, diarrhoea, and even death, especially in kittens. Vaccination against feline infectious enteritis is extremely effective and provides prolonged protection.

Cat flu

Feline herpesvirus (FHV-1) and feline calicivirus (FCV) are spread by close contact with carriers, and are responsible for the majority of cases of acute upper respiratory tract disease, or "cat flu". Infection causes mild to severe signs including sore throat (pharyngitis), mouth ulcers, coughing, sneezing, nasal discharge, and eye inflammation and discharge. Pneumonia is a life-threatening complication. Some cats recover fully in a few days; others take weeks, or suffer permanent damage to the nose or eyes.

Vaccination protects a cat from severe illness but does not prevent infection. Even more exasperating, vaccinated cats can still become carriers of the viruses and pass them on to others, but show no signs of disease themselves.

Feline leukemia virus (FeLV)

This is a fragile virus transmitted via the saliva in prolonged close contact between cats. Infection usually results in life-long infection and, frustratingly, most cats die within three years of being diagnosed with FeLV, usually from an associated illness such as lymphoma or anaemia.

Only around 1 per cent of healthy cats test positive; up to 18 per cent of ill cats seen by vets have FeLV. Blood testing has been very effective in reducing incidence in pedigree cat breeding. FeLV vaccine provides protection for cats at risk, but it doesn't necessarily protect all cats.

Left *Cat flu is forcing this cat to breathe through its mouth because its nostrils are blocked. This is more likely in flat-faced cats with already small nostrils.*

Right *Flu viruses cause eye inflammation, as here, where the "third eyelids" are both visible and inflamed. The cat is obviously unhappy and needs attention.*

Combined flu and enteritis inoculations are usually given under the skin in the scruff.

Rabies This virus attacks the central nervous system and causes fatal disease. Rabies virus can infect almost all warm-blooded animals, but is most common in members of the canine family, cats, bats, and monkeys. The virus is excreted into saliva and can be transmitted to humans, usually through bites.

Vaccination, which is mandatory in some localities or for travelling cats, provides efficient and effective protection, often for three or more years.

How I vaccinate

I vaccinate all kittens against feline infectious enteritis, and the cat flu viruses feline herpesvirus-1 (FHV-1) and feline calicivirus (FCV). The American Academy of Feline Medicine and the American Association of Feline Practitioners jointly recommend that after a first annual booster vaccination, cats should be vaccinated no more often than every three years for feline infectious enteritis, and in general every three years for FHV 1 and FCV. I follow their guidelines, but boarding catteries often require proof of vaccination within the preceding 12 months.

Outdoor cats that meet feral cats are vaccinated against FeLV when young, but

not when they are older. Where travel requirements stipulate, I vaccinate cats against rabies.

Vaccinations I don't give

There are diseases I don't vaccinate against, for a range of reasons. They include the following infections.

Bordetella bronchiseptica

This is a significant cause of "kennel cough" in dogs and can sometimes cause sneezing and nasal discharge in cats.

Although an intra-nasal vaccine for cats is available, infection is usually self-limiting and responds well to antibiotics.

Feline chlamydophilosis

Once called *Chlamydophila felis*, this causes severe, prolonged conjunctivitis that responds to antibiotics (*see* page 156). It is transmitted by direct contact between cats and is most common in kittens from multi-cat households.

Vaccination provides protection from severe illness but does not necessarily prevent infection. I only use this in known high-risk situations.

Feline coronavirus (FCoV)

This infects 80 to 100 per cent of cats from breeding catteries and large colonies. For reasons that are not understood, in

rare instances FCoV causes fatal feline infectious peritonitis or FIP, usually in youngsters between six months and two years of age. The Persian and Burmese breeds may be more genetically susceptible than others.

The early clinical signs of FIP are non-specific – fluctuating fever, lethargy, loss of appetite, weight loss, diarrhoea, and occasionally mild upper respiratory tract signs – but eventually fluid accumulates in the abdomen. Blood testing for FIP is frustrating, because no simple test differentiates between the mild and relatively insignificant strain of FCoV, present in so many cats, and the lethal strain that causes FIP.

An intranasal vaccine is available in many parts of the world, but its usefulness is questionable. The vaccine is currently licensed only for use in kittens over 16 weeks of age, but in endemic situations most kittens of this age will already be infected with FCoV. I can't recommend routine vaccination.

Feline immunodeficiency virus (FIV)

This is surprisingly common among free-ranging cats. Many infected cats survive in good health, although they transmit the virus to other cats, and the virus can cause very serious disease. Surveys of cats brought to vets suggest that 10–20 per cent of sick cats have been exposed to FIV, usually through bites or repeated social licking.

The first signs of infection are non-specific – fever, lethargy, and possibly lymph node enlargement. Good health returns, but then other very variable signs of disease may develop, including weight loss, gum disease, loss of appetite, intermittent fever, conjunctivitis, sneezing, or tumours.

Kittens usually lose inherited protection from diseases by ten weeks of age. Protection is perpetuated through the efficient and sensible use of safe vaccines.

A vaccine against FIV is licensed in the United States, but academic researchers question its value.

Giardia is a common cause of chronic diarrhoea. A vaccine against it is available in the United States, but Canadian studies suggest it does not reduce the amount of infectious material the cat sheds in its faeces. As giardia usually responds to simple medications, I don't recommend its use.

Vaccine reactions
Mild reactions, such as pain at the injection site or a low fever for a day, are neither unusual nor worrying, but more severe adverse reactions to inoculations do sometimes occur. In the largest British published survey, suspected adverse reactions occured in one out of every 15,000 inoculations, usually in cats under six months old. These included:
- Lameness/polyarthritis (18 per cent)
- Local injection site reactions (16 per cent)
- Allergic reactions, such as anaphylaxis and hypersensitivity (9 per cent)
- Lack of efficacy (6 per cent)
- Upper respiratory tract disease (6 per cent)
- Sarcomas (3 per cent)

Injection sarcomas
While 3 per cent of the reported suspected adverse reactions to injections are tumours called sarcomas, recent research suggests that the vaccination itself does not cause the sarcoma. Instead, the tumour develops in some cats as a result of that individual's genetic predisposition to develop sarcomas after inflammation from any cause. Vaccination, other injections, and even other forms of trauma may all cause inflammation leading to the growth of a sarcoma. There is no difference in the likelihood of injection site sarcomas for products from different vaccine manufacturers. Other studies have shown injection-site sarcomas can develop after the injection of other products, including antibiotics, to some cats.

The tumour is devastating for the cat affected, but the true incidence of injection-site sarcomas is considerably lower than some 1990s estimates, probably around 1 in 10,000 to 30,000.

Cats pass infections to us

While most infectious diseases can only be transmitted within a species, there are some agents that can cross species boundaries and pass from animals to people. Cats can carry a range of these infections, although the risks are smaller than many articles suggest.

Ringworm

Ringworm is a fungal infection, and its spores survive for prolonged periods in the soil. If spores caught in cat hair infect a cat's skin, they produce circular skin lesions, hence the name ringworm. Spores can be transmitted to us without actually infecting the cat, so although your cat may be disease-free, it is still capable of transmitting ringworm (*see* page 154).

If your cat has ringworm, avoid unnecessary handling. Prevent children, who are particularly susceptible to infection, from touching it. Wear disposable gloves when in contact with your cat while you carry out your vet's instructions to wash it in an antifungal shampoo and treat with antifungal tablets. If you have ringworm, assume your cat is a carrier, even if it is disease free, and follow your vet's advice on treating your home as well as your cat.

It can be particularly difficult to wholly eliminate ringworm from a household with numerous longhaired cats.

Bite and scratch infections

Cat bites are surprisingly common. Most cause only minor inconvenience, but some, particularly those contaminated by the bacteria *Pasteurella multocida*, cause painful, swollen reactions, even abscesses (*see* page 155). Cat scratches are even more common, and sometimes transmit a bacteria called *Bartonella henselae*. This can cause systemic illness called "cat scratch fever"; symptoms include enlarged lymph nodes, particularly in children three to twelve years old and people with impaired immune systems.

Wash any wounds with antibacterial soap and seek medical advice if bitten.

Fleas

Fleas just love cats, and most cats are not bothered by minor flea infestations (*see* pages 152–3). Fleas enjoy meals from us too, often snacking on our ankles, causing bites that look and feel like mosquito bites. Fleas spread *Bartonella henselae* (*see* bite and scratch infections above) to cats.

Cats that venture outdoors should be routinely treated with modern "spot-on"

Cats do not directly transmit toxoplasmosis to pregnant women. Even so, if you are pregnant use sensible precautions to protect your developing baby.

flea prevention products. Your home will also need treatment, because fleas can live separately from a host for many months.

Toxoplasmosis

Around 50 per cent of all outdoor cats have been infected with *Toxoplasma gondii* at some point in their lives. This parasite can cause developmental problems to the growing human foetus, including blindness and increased risk of developing allergies and asthma.

A few days after a cat has been infected for the first time by eating meat containing the parasite, it will start to shed millions of eggs in its faeces. This continues for around 14 days, before the body's immune response stops further egg production. These eggs, or oocysts, can survive in the soil or water for up to 18 months, even in extreme weather conditions. Other animals, including our livestock, become infected by swallowing oocysts, and this infection results in formation of tissue cysts in various tissues of the body. We contract the infection by contact with oocysts, either in the cat's faeces or – much more commonly – by eating meat containing these oocysts.

The foetuses of women who have not been infected prior to pregnancy are particularly vulnerable to toxoplasma-induced disease if the mother is infected while pregnant. The effects of infection are most severe when infection occurs between months two and six of gestation. If a woman already has antibodies to *T. gondii* before she becomes pregnant there is no risk that the infection can be passed on to the fetus.

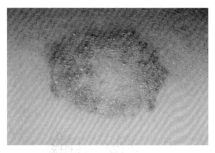

Ringworm, which causes circular, sometimes itchy, sores on our skin, can be transmitted to us by a cat that acts only as a carrier, and is not itself infected.

Human and dog fleas are uncommon, even rare, but cat fleas are ubiquitous, and happy to snack off anyone. If you are bitten by a flea, it is most likely to be a cat flea.

BRUCE'S CAT CONTACT AND TOXOPLASMOSIS TIP

Antibodies to the toxoplasma parasite develop following infection. Contact with cats has no influence on the probability of people having antibodies to the parasite; consuming raw meat does. That's why only 20 per cent of people in the United Kingdom have antibodies to toxo, while 80 per cent of French and Germans, who eat more raw or undercooked meat, do. Vets working with cats don't have a higher incidence of protective antibodies than the general population, including people not in contact with cats. Stroking a cat will not spread infection from cats to people.

Reducing the risk of toxo

Toxoplasma is more likely to be contracted from eating undercooked meat than from contact with cat faeces during the two-week period in which the parasite is viable after the cat's first consumption of contaminated wildlife. If you are pregnant, you can reduce the risks in several ways.

- Wear gloves when handling raw meat and wash your hands after.
- Eat only thoroughly cooked meat or meat that has been smoked, cured, or frozen for at least three days.
- Wash vegetables and fruit thoroughly before eating.
- Wear rubber gloves when gardening.

Reducing the risk from your cat

Although the risk of direct transmission of the parasite from a house cat to a person is very low, this can be reduced further in the following ways.

- Feed only properly cooked food or commercial cat food to your cat to avoid infection.

- Keep cats off kitchen work surfaces.
- Wear gloves when cleaning the cat's litter tray, or get someone else to do it.
- Dispose of cat litter safely by sealing it in a plastic bag before putting it with other household waste.
- Cover children's sandpits when not in use to prevent cats from using them as litter trays.

If you are particularly concerned, ask your vet to check your cat's toxoplasma titre. Cats with a positive titre have been infected in the past and will not be a source of infection in the future, because they have completed their period of oocyst shedding.

Diseases that cats don't pass to us

Cats are frequently and erroneously blamed for transmitting a variety of diseases, infections, or infestations to people. Even medical doctors inaccurately accuse household cats of being the source of a variety of conditions. These include:

Roundworms

Many books and websites state that we are prone to infection from the cat roundworm *Toxocara cati*. We are not. Transmission is extremely rare. Children are, however, prone to infection from the dog roundworm *Toxocara canis*. (Some "experts" also state that dog roundworms frequently cause blindness. They do not. Dog roundworms can cause reduced vision in one eye and exceptionally the loss of vision in a single eye, but never total blindness.)

Gastric ulcers

Helicobacter pylori is a bacteria that causes gastric ulcers in people. A helicobacter organism has been found in cat stomachs, and it has been suggested that cats

transmit this organism to people. There is no evidence, either statistical or medical, that this is true. Cat owners do not suffer from any higher incidence of helicobacter-induced gastric ulcers than people who do not own cats.

Fresh-water diarrhoea

Giardia causes diarrhoea in both cats and people. Cats don't transmit giardia to us. We both contract the infection from the same contaminated water. Giardia is the cause of what is called "beaver fever" in North America; diarrhoea contracted by drinking untreated water on canoe trips.

HIV

The feline immune deficiency virus (FIV, *see* page 136) and human immune deficiency virus (HIV) may have similar names, but they are completely different viruses. FIV does not cause AIDS or other disease in people.

Leukemia

Feline leukemia virus (FeLV, *see* page 135) causes leukemia, lymphoma, and immune system failure in cats, but there is no evidence that it is associated with similar conditions in people. Vets are frequently exposed to this feline virus, but we do not have an increased incidence of any of these conditions.

Avian and swine flu

Cats can become infected with the H5N1 avian flu virus, and it killed several cats in Germany and Austria. However, cats are not important carriers of this virus; they excrete less than one-thousandth of the amount of virus that chickens do. In the United States, in a rare instance, swine flu was transmitted from humans to a cat, but not vice versa.

Use sensible parasite control

A variety of both internal and external parasites have evolved to live, often in peaceful harmony, with cats. A few are potentially transmissible to us, or are certainly happy to live on or in us. Fortunately, advances in parasite control mean that it is fairly simple to prevent, or treat, almost any infestation through topical treatments or tablets. Outdoor cats need routine preventative treatment.

- **Roundworms** are often inherited by kittens either via the placenta or in the first milk. The size of small earthworms, they may be vomited or seen in faeces.
- **Tapeworms** are mostly contracted by eating infected fleas. Rice-grain-sized segments are passed from the anus.
- **Hookworms and whipworms** are both rare in cats, but can cause watery to bloody diarrhoea.
- **Giardia** is a single-cell protozoan parasite contracted by drinking contaminated water. It causes chronically loose stools.
- **Heartworms** are transmitted through mosquito bites and can clog the heart and major blood vessels, reducing capacity to exercise. They occur throughout Eastern North America and much of continental Europe.
- **Fleas** leave black, shiny specks of dirt in the coat, and sometimes their eggs too. They are the most common cause of feline skin and coat problems (*see* pages

BRUCE'S LICKING TIP

If your cat is licking its bum excessively, think of the possibility of tapeworms but also check that its anal sacs are not blocked. This becomes a greater cause of bum licking as cats get older.

DECLAWING IS NOT HEALTHY

The surgical removal of all the claws on a cat's forepaws is routine in some countries but holds no benefits for a cat. It is done for us, to save our furniture or carpets from being scratched. Regardless of how much painkiller is used, or how efficient the anaesthetist and surgeon are, declawing is painful and is riskier than being left alone. Be humane to your cat. Cut its nails to keep them blunt, and provide suitable scratching posts where it can carry out its natural need to scratch, but don't amputate its claws for your own convenience.

152–5). Treat your household with flea-birth-control and flea-killer products to prevent reinfestation.

- **Ear mites** produce gritty, sandy debris in the ears, and are often contracted from mothers or neighbouring cats.
- **Ticks** attach themselves to places where cats find it hard to lick. They gorge on blood for several days then drop off. Ticks carry a variety of potentially serious diseases.

All of these parasites are eliminated using a variety of prescription antihelmintics. Some spot-ons kill virtually all of them.

Neutering prolongs life expectancy

Although we neuter cats because it is such an effective way of both ensuring birth control and eliminating the more unpleasant aspects (at least to us) of reproductive behaviours, neutering females, in particular, has a dramatic effect on health. Neutering before the first season eliminates the risk of breast cancer, a common form of feline cancer. It also eliminates the risk of pyometra, a potentially life-threatening infection in the womb. Neutered female cats live

BRUCE'S SPOT-ON TIP

Take extreme care when using spot-on products. Some contain permethrins, licensed for use only on dogs and potentially lethal to cats. Read labels carefully: the warnings about dangers to cats are often in much smaller print than they should be.

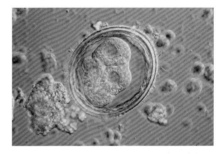

Top *Cats can carry a variety of intestinal parasites. An examination of a stool sample under a microscope can reveal worm eggs such as this roundworm egg.*

Bottom *Tapeworms grow to a considerable size, but all we usually see at the cat's anus are individual egg-sac segments. The size of rice grains, these drop off from the thicker end of the worm.*

considerably longer than unneutered individuals. Neutered males fight less, and the consequence is less risk of contracting life-threatening viral conditions such as FIV and FeLV and less risk of bite infections and their complications. Neutering is a simple and effective way to help maintain your cat's good health.

Choose a vet sensibly

Cost and proximity are not the only factors when selecting a vet for your cat. In the best of circumstances the two of you should have similar attitudes towards ethical issues, such as declawing, as well as preventative measures including the frequency of inoculations and worming. Concerning cost, in most instances we do get what we pay for. An extensive range of diagnostic equipment increases costs within a clinic but also increases the ability to make efficient diagnoses. When choosing a vet, ask to have a look

Both you and your cat should feel comfortable with the vets and the veterinary staff who you will be in contact with for practical advice and medical care.

around and to meet the staff. If staff stay for decades you're often assured that both the medical and ethical standards of the practice are excellent.

Kittens do happen

Many of the kittens I see at the clinic are the result of their mothers' unauthorized assignations. Early neutering avoids unwanted kittens, but if you think your cat might be pregnant check her nipples. These become more prominent and pinker by three weeks of gestation. By four to five weeks after conception your vet will be able to feel golf-ball-sized swellings in her abdomen. Shortly after, her belly becomes visibly enlarged. Pregnancy lasts about nine weeks.

Giving birth

Birth is usually uncomplicated. In her chosen secluded, warm den the mother digs at the surface, often purring rhythmically. Soon her breathing quickens and the contractions of labour begin. Once contractions occur every 30 seconds, a delivery is imminent. About 70 per cent of kittens are born in a diving, head-and-feet first position. Good mothers instinctively lick away the membranes and in doing so stimulate each kitten to take its first breath. The mother consumes all birth wastes in her efforts to prevent predators from knowing

there is a litter of helpless kittens. A powerful instinct may also drive her to remove her new litter from danger. She picks up each kitten by the scruff and carries it to a new, safer nest. When "scruffed" the kitten instinctively stops wriggling and draws all its legs close to its body to prevent them from being injured during transport. The scruff response remains intact throughout a cat's life.

Above *Cats frequently give birth in our own homes, and usually there are no complications. Ensure that your cat has a clean, secure, and quiet location in which she can raise her litter.*

Below left *The great majority of cats instinctively and successfully clear away (and eat) the birth membranes and chew off the umbilical cord.*

Below right *At birth a kitten has a heat-seeking ability to find its mother, warmth, and nourishment. The other senses rapidly develop in the following weeks.*

This isn't just cute: mothers continue to groom their kittens for social reasons. It bonds them together and is also the reason why cats like to be stroked by us.

> ### BRUCE'S TIPS FOR RAISING BETTER KITTENS
>
> - Ensure that mothers are "emotionally competent" to raise their kittens. Never breed from young females who have not reached emotional maturity.
> - Offer balanced nourishment to the mother while she is pregnant and during her period of milk production. Good nourishment is necessary for proper physical and mental development.
> - Allow kittens to continue to suckle right up to twelve weeks of age, for proper social development.
> - Handle kittens frequently, especially from birth to seven weeks, and expose them to mild sensory stimulations.
> - Think of how the kitten will live as an adult, and introduce other different species early in life.

The first weeks

During the first few weeks of life, a kitten depends upon its mother to stimulate all its body functions. Her licking prompts the kitten to release its bladder and bowels, and just as she tidied her nest at birth, she also consumes all of her kitten's body waste products to hide her litter's presence from predators. A kitten is capable of fully grooming itself at five weeks old, but still depends upon its mother for most of its grooming.

Suckling for nourishment lasts for five to six weeks but continues for emotional benefits for an equal length of time. For the first few weeks the mother induces her kittens to suckle, but then they begin to pester her for a meal. At three weeks of age a kitten starts to eat solid food, and by five weeks it has a full set of pin-sharp milk teeth.

Handle kittens frequently

Early and routine handling, especially and vitally from three to seven weeks of age, produces adult cats that head- and flank-rub more and chirp and purr more when humans approach. Routine handling also helps kittens grow faster and possibly bigger. If social contact with people does not begin until after seven weeks, kittens develop into more withdrawn adults. Equally important, calm mothers, at ease with people, teach their kittens to be equally at ease in the presence of such potentially intimidating predators.

Sensitive periods in development

Kittens develop their social manners between three and seven weeks of age. If during this time a kitten frequently meets members of another species – dogs or rats or horses or humans – it will develop a social rapport with that species and not look upon it as predator or prey. That's at the very heart of a contented co-existence. If a cat does not learn at this early stage how to live in harmony with us or with other animals, natural fears are likely to develop.

If your kitten comes to depend upon you for food, security, and warmth through early learning, it will probably think of you as its mother for its lifetime, which is the essence of your relationship.

Know your cat's routines

Cats develop routines, and any change means something has happened. In many instances a break in routines is triggered by a social change, for example a new cat arriving on its territory, but illness also affects routines. Most of us know our cats' routines; monitor what your cat does.

Sleep

Cats sleep longer than many other species but, like us, they have different types of sleep routines. These range from resting with the eyes closed, to sleep from which they are easily aroused, to deep sleep.

Thinking time

When your cat is awake, even if it is indoors, it will patrol its territory. It will rest, both in an alert way with its eyes open and in an absent way as if its mind is somewhere else. It will look out of windows. It will visit its (usually elevated) observation points.

Outdoor activities

If your cat goes outdoors it patrols its territory, marking it, hunting on it, and interacting with people, dogs, or other cats on it.

Eating

Some cats graze on their food, especially if it is dry food and there's no competition. Others are furry vacuum cleaners.

Grooming

Your cat ritually grooms, typically after eating and toileting, but almost always

Cats naturally sleep much more than we do or dogs do. It's good for them, but just seeing a sleeping cat, upside down on a bed, makes us feel better too.

following a set pattern that lasts for what is generally a pre-determined time.

Social activity and play

Your cat has a routine in how it plays with its toys or other objects. It also ritually initiates or demands play or attention from other pets or from you.

Changes to look out for

If there are changes in any of these activities that you cannot with certainty attribute to changes in the environment, your cat may not be feeling well. There also may be other changes.

Temperament or behaviour

- Reluctance to be handled
- Unexpected or unusual threats or other signs of aggression, either to you or to the other cats
- Unexpected fearful behaviour
- Hiding

Gait and posture

- Obvious lameness
- Stiffness when walking
- An arched back or tucked up belly
- Unexpected resting on the chest and unwillingness to get up
- More tentative than normal jumping

Breathing

- Unexpected panting
- Heavy breathing from the belly rather than from the chest
- Faster breathing than normal
- Breathing out looks harder than breathing in or vice versa

Facial expression

- Glazed look to the eyes
- Furrowed brow
- Hanging head

Vocalising

- Greater or less than normal
- Any changes to normal sounds
- Any new sounds

General behaviours

- Scratching more than normal
- Drinking more or less
- Changes in elimination habits

Signs of serious conditions

If your cat is not behaving normally, carry out a few quick checks to start with.

Check the gums

The normal colour is pink. Pale to white gums may indicate shock or anaemia, blue gums indicate not enough oxygen, yellow gums indicate liver problems, and bright red can indicate carbon monoxide poisoning or heatstroke.

Check hydration

Check for dehydration by grasping some skin at the back of their neck (the scruff) and gently pulling it up. In the well-hydrated cat, the skin springs back immediately. In a dehydrated cat, the skin will be slower to retract. The more severe the dehydration, the longer the skin will take to retract.

BRUCE'S TIPS

Cats hide that they are unwell. Simple changes often indicate serious illness. Any of these warrant immediate contact with your vet.

Behaviour	Possible problem
Abnormal breathing	Fluid in the chest cavity Heart failure Asthma Lung disease Heat stroke
Unsteady on its feet	Poisoning Neurological disorder Ear infection Spinal trauma Pelvis fracture Brain trauma
Bad breath	Kidney disease Diabetes mellitus Liver disease Tooth abscess Periodontal disease Intestinal problems Cancers of the mouth
Loss of appetite	Infections and abscesses Injuries and trauma Mouth pain or gastrointestintal conditions Dehydration Anaemia
Drinking more	Diabetes Kidney failure Lower urinary tract disorder Urinary tract infection Womb infection Overactive thyroid

Check circulation

Check "capillary refill time". This helps you check your cat's blood circulation. To test capillary refill time, lift your cat's upper lip and press the flat of your finger against the gum tissue. Remove your finger and you will see a white mark on the gum where your finger was placed. Time how long it takes for the pink colour to return to the white spot. In the healthy cat it should take around a second to return to pink. Slower return of colour can mean dehydration, heart failure, or shock from any cause.

Accidents do happen

When an accident happens, stay calm and assess the dangers to make sure you don't put yourself in danger, then restrain your cat, check its heart and breathing, look for signs of shock, and if all of these systems are in order, arrange for care of any physical injuries such as puncture wounds or broken bones. You will probably never need to use life-saving skills on your cat, but that doesn't mean these skills aren't useful.

BRUCE'S HANDLING TIP

It is always much easier and faster for a vet to make a diagnosis on a cat that willingly allows itself to be examined. Train your cat at home, using rewards, to allow a full examination of its body.

Catch and inspect your cat

Calmly approach your cat, trying not to frighten it. Talk reassuringly and avoid intimidating eye contact. Gently wrap it in a large towel or any other soft material. Lift it away from further danger, then gently unwrap the head while keeping the rest of the body safely cocooned so it cannot lash out with claws or teeth. Carry out a quick inspection. Check breathing: cats normally breathe in and out about 30 times a minute. Breathing rates increase with pain, shock, and lung or heart problems. Breathing and panting are different: panting occurs with anxiety, pain or to get rid of excess heat.

Check the heart rate

Your cat's normal resting pulse rate is about 120 beats a minute, increasing to 200 beats per minute when frightened.

When accidents happen, wrapping your cat conserves warmth and prevents any further damage while you arrange to get it to the vet.

BRUCE'S TEMPERATURE TIP

When a cat is unwell, warmth is vital. As well as ensuring that your cat does not become dehydrated and eats what your vet suggests is best, keep its environment cosy and warm. Keep outdoor cats indoors where there is heat and no draughts. If your cat finds a favoured hiding place to rest in ensure it is as warm as, even a little warmer than, the rest of your home.

A kitten's heart may beat over 200 times a minute. The rate increases with fever, pain, heart conditions and in the first stages of shock. To monitor the heart,

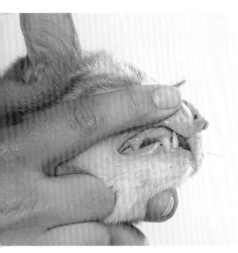

If your cat seems unwell, check the colour of the gums. They should be a healthy pink; if they are either white or blue, get immediate veterinary attention.

CPR MAY BE NEEDED IN THESE CIRCUMSTANCES

- Blood loss
- Choking
- Concussion
- Diabetic coma
- Electrocution
- Heart failure
- Near-drowning
- Poisoning
- Shock
- Smoke inhalation
- Severe allergic reactions

BRUCE'S BREATHING TIP

An unconscious cat sometimes breathes so gently it is difficult to see. If you are not sure whether your cat is breathing, hold a mirror close to its nose and look for condensation. If this is present, your cat is breathing. Alternatively, hold a small piece of tissue or cotton wool in front of the nostrils and watch for any movement that indicates shallow breathing.

grasp the chest on both sides, just behind the elbows, and squeeze gently until you feel heartbeats. This may be difficult to do on very fat cats. Alternatively, feel the pulse by placing your fingers inside the hind leg where it meets the groin. The femoral artery passes through here. Move your fingers around until you pick up its pulse: this is easier if you do it regularly.

Never underestimate shock

Shock is a silent killer. Controlling shock takes precedence over first aid for other injuries such as broken bones. A cat may look fine after an accident, then die a few hours later of clinical shock.

Signs of early shock

- Faster than normal breathing, sometimes panting
- Faster than normal pounding heart rate
- Pale gums
- Anxiety or restlessness
- Lethargy and weakness
- Normal (37.8–38.9°C/100–102°F) or subnormal rectal temperature
- Slow capillary refill time to the gums – more than two seconds

Signs of late shock

- Shallow, irregular breathing
- Irregular heart beat
- Very pale or blue gums and dilated eyes
- Extreme weakness or unconsciousness
- Very cool body temperature, especially the paws, of less than 36.7°C (98°F).
- Very slow capillary refill time to the gums – more than four seconds

These signs indicate that heart failure and death are imminent.

If your cat shows signs of shock

- Don't let it wander about or give anything to eat or drink.

- Stop any bleeding and give heart massage or artificial respiration as necessary.
- Wrap the cat in a blanket to prevent further heat loss.
- Use pillows or towels to elevate the hindquarters, allowing more blood to travel to the brain.
- Keep the head extended and transport to your nearest vet immediately.

Giving cardiopulmonary resuscitation (CPR)

In emergencies, heart massage can restart a stopped heart, while artificial respiration puts oxygen back into your cat's lungs. The combination of heart massage and artificial respiration is called cardiopulmonary resuscitation, or CPR.

When and how to give artificial respiration

Give artificial respiration only if your cat has stopped breathing. Pink gums usually mean that oxygen is being carried around the body. If they are blue or white, artificial respiration may be necessary.

If your cat has stopped breathing, take the following steps:

- Place the cat on its side, clear any debris from the nose and mouth, and pull the tongue forward.
- Close the mouth and, with the neck in a straight line, place your mouth over its nose, and blow in until you see the chest expand. If you find this offensive, use your hand to form an airtight cylinder between your mouth and your cat's nose. Blow through this.
- Take your mouth away. The lungs will naturally deflate. Repeat this procedure 10 to 20 times a minute, until the cat breathes on its own.

- Check the pulse every 15 seconds to ensure the heart is still beating. If it stops, integrate heart massage with artificial respiration.
- Get emergency veterinary help as soon as possible.

When and how to give heart massage

Only give heart massage if your cat's heart is not beating. Check the eyes: they dilate when the heart stops. Feel for a heartbeat or pulse, and check the gums. If there is no pulse and the gums do not refill with blood, the heart has stopped.

If the heart has stopped, take the following steps:
- Place your cat on its side, if possible with its head at a lower level than the rest of the body.

- Grasp the chest, behind the elbows, between your fingers and thumb. Support the back with your other hand.
- Squeeze firmly, compressing the ribcage up towards the neck. Repeat,using quick, firm pumps, 120 times a minute.
- After 15 seconds of heart massage, give artificial respiration for 10 seconds.

Oxygen is routinely given through an oxygen mask like this during operations. At home, in emergencies, you can give mouth-to-mouth artificial respiration.

- Continue alternating until a pulse returns, then continue to give artificial respiration alone.
- Get immediate veterinary attention.

TEMPERATURE RANGE

°C	°F	
41+	106+	Heat stroke: cool down immediately; get urgent veterinary attention
40.6	105	Dangerous: seek same day veterinary attention
40.0	104	High fever: seek same day veterinary advice
39.4	103	Moderate fever: telephone veterinarian for advice
38.9	102	Normal
38.3	101	Normal
37.8	100	Normal
37.2	99	Sub-normal: seek same day veterinary advice
36.7-	98-	Hypothermia: keep cat warm; get urgent veterinary attention

Excess weight and diabetes

It may be a consequence of our affection for our cats, but obesity is the most common form of malnutrition I see in clinical practice. Around one in three of all cats, especially indoor cats, is either overweight or clinically obese. Obesity leads to increased pain in older age and shortens life expectancy. It's the most common factor in diabetes in younger cats. And it's completely avoidable, because it's caused by you!

Lifestyle affects weight

Of course, it's no different with cats than it is with us. Consume more calories than you burn up in exercise each day, and the excess energy gets converted to fat and stored for the day you find yourself on an Arctic ice floe with nothing to eat.

We increase the cat's already excellent ability to conserve energy by neutering them: when a cat is neutered, the metabolic rate decreases by about 20 per cent, so neutered cats require less food. Neutering also reduces the desire to roam, so the amount of daily activity declines.

Living indoors makes things even worse. With restricted opportunities for exercise, cats use up even less energy, so they gain weight. It's no surprise that cats under two years of age are less likely to be overweight than cats between two and ten years. What is surprising to me is that purebred cats are somehow less likely to develop obesity than moggies.

Watch that diet

Obesity increases the risks of skin disease (*see* pages 152–3), lower urinary tract disease (*see* pages 170–1), arthritis (*see* pages 172–4), and sugar diabetes. "Reducing" diets that are high in protein, low in fat, and low in carbohydrate, help cats to lose fat while maintaining good muscle mass. When using any diet, aim for a gradual decrease in bodyweight, up to a year for a very obese cat to reach its ideal body condition. Too fast a loss of weight can cause severe liver disease.

Diabetes

Diabetes affects around one in 200 cats – and is increasing. Obesity is the most common trigger, so the easiest way to prevent diabetes is to prevent obesity. It's as simple as that. Routine health checks including urine checks help pick up early signs of diabetes. When diabetic cats are treated correctly and early, as many as 50–60 per cent recover. That means their diabetes is transient; you don't need to give insulin for the rest of your cat's life. Frustratingly, it's not possible to predict which cats will fall into this category.

Bruce's weigh tip

It's very hard to see gradual weight loss in a cat. Weigh-ins every two to three weeks ensure that weight loss is occurring and is not too rapid. Once your cat has reached its target weight, feed a "light" or low-calorie food. Creative manufacturers use words like "neutered cat" for these diets.

ASSESS YOUR CAT'S BODY CONDITION

Vets use a scale called the Body Condition Score or BCS to assess whether a cat is overweight or obese; you can too. BCS grades your cat's body from 1 to 5.

1 **Very thin**
2 **Thin**
3 **Ideal**
   Waist can be seen behind the ribs
   Minimal abdominal fat
   Hip bones covered in thin layer of fat
   Slight fat cover over ribs
4 **Overweight**
   Waist hardly discernible
   Moderate abdominal fat
   Hip bones can be felt but covered by moderate layer of fat
   Ribs not easily felt
5 **Obese**
   No waist, distended abdomen
   Extensive abdominal fat
   Hip bones difficult to feel because of fat
   Ribs cannot be felt because of thick fat

The cat on the left is in ideal shape: a visible neck, no surplus abdominal fat, and placing its forepaws easily side by side. The centre cat is overweight and needs a 10–15 per cent cut in energy intake. The cat on the right is obese, and needs a cut of at least 20 per cent in intake.

As well as assessing your cat's BCS, weigh it routinely. If your cat is gaining weight or weighs more that your vet says is healthy, it needs a calorie controlled diet; remember, obesity shortens life expectancy.

Weight management

If you have a diabetic or overweight cat, involve everyone who cares for your cat.

Weigh out your cat's daily high-protein, low-carbohydrate food each morning and place it in a container to divide between the allocated meals. This way you are less likely to overfeed. Use a few kibbles as treats throughout the day, but give no "extras" – and remember, extras include milk and cat milk!

If you have more than one cat, feed them separately and watch over them when they eat. Give diabetic cats insulin injections twice daily. Remember to tell your neighbours that your cat is diabetic and should not be fed.

Increase exercise by using toys, light torches, and other items your cat enjoys. Remember, little and often is best. If you wish, place food in different areas or hide kibbles around the house to encourage more exercise. A food ball or "puzzle" feeder is useful, because it makes your cat work a little for its food.

Above *The clouded appearance of the lens in the eye is a cataract. A cataract in one eye may result from an injury, but bilateral cataracts are often a consequence of untreated diabetes.*

Right *Giving cats insulin is easier than you might think and rarely resented, especially if combined with treats.*

Skin conditions

Skin problems are the most common reason why cats are taken to vets. Most skin problems involve itchiness, and most of that itchiness is caused by fleas. Put that together and it may be that cat fleas are the single most common (and avoidable) reason cats are treated by vets. Of course there are other skin problems, primarily abscesses from cat fights, but also infections such as ringworm and even skin tumours.

Miliary dermatitis and flea allergy

Miliary dermatitis is a condition where tiny scabs develop anywhere on the cat's body. The coat often becomes either greasy or dandruffy. The most common cause of miliary dermatitis is fleas, although it can also be caused by food allergies and other skin parasites such as the cheyletiella mite.

Flea allergy dermatitis is a form of miliary dermatitis that occurs when a cat has an itchy, inflammatory response to flea saliva. Just one bite from one flea, once, can trigger flea allergy dermatitis. This is the most common allergy cats suffer from. In temperate climates, flea allergy dermatitis occurs most often in the summer and autumn, because cooler temperatures and low humidity inhibit flea development, while in warmer climates it persists year round.

Miliary dermatitis is itchy

A cat with miliary dermatitis constantly grooms itself but also scratches, bites, and licks, causing damage to the skin. This is what causes the small crusts or scabs.

Hair loss may occur, usually on the rump and extending up the back or on the belly between the hind legs. Secondary bacterial and yeast infections are common in chronic cases, and these create an unpleasant odour.

Scab pattern helps diagnosis

The pattern of scabs suggests what the cause of miliary dermatitis is. Scabs along the midline of the back and around the neck suggest an allergy to fleas. Flea allergy dermatitis can also cause hair loss over the rump area, which then extends along the midline of the back, towards the neck. The skin in this area may be thickened, darker than usual, or irritated from scratching and chewing. Miliary scabs associated with food allergies tend to concentrate over the head and tail regions. Food allergies can also lead to circular sores, mainly on the head, neck, and shoulders. Food allergies, by the way, don't usually cause diarrhoea in cats.

Prevention and treatment

Eliminate fleas, the most common cause of miliary dermatitis, by using an efficient topical flea killer such as Frontline, Advantage, or Stronghold. Treat the cat's environment with thorough vacuuming and sprays that stop flea eggs from developing. A short course of cortisone may be needed to stop self-inflicted damage, or antibiotics to eliminate secondary bacterial or yeast infections. The only long-term treatment for flea allergy dermatitis is total flea control and not allowing one single flea to come in contact with your cat. Desensitizing shots do not seem to work well for controlling flea allergy dermatitis.

If miliary dermatitis persists after fleas are completely eliminated, consider food allergies. Feed a novel-protein or low-allergenic diet for at least four to six weeks. If after three weeks the skin starts to improve, then miliary dermatitis has been caused by diet.

Eosinophilic granuloma complex

Three inflammatory skin conditions called eosinophilic ulcer, eosinophilic plaque, and eosinophilic granuloma are grouped together as "eosinophilic granuloma complex". Flea, food, or environmental allergy plays a role in these skin conditions. The complicated name actually describes the problem: eosinophils are white blood cells mobilized by the body's immune system to react to the presence of something foreign. When they are sent to a particular spot of skin, inflammation occurs. Normally they do their job and then leave, but sometimes they remain in the area for long periods, and the inflammation develops into a lump or "granuloma". If the lump occurs on the upper lip near a canine tooth it is called an eosinophilic or rodent ulcer. Although these look sensitive, they are not usually painful or itchy. The lesion starts off as a lump but can become ulcerated if the cat licks it a lot. Licking with the rough feline tongue causes more damage than the granuloma itself. Ulcerated, scaly eosinophilic plaques occur on the cat's stomach and inner thigh. Often seen in two to six year olds, these are made worse by constant licking. All of these conditions are probably an allergic response to something as yet unknown.

> **BRUCE'S HAIR LOSS TIP**
>
> In humans and dogs, hair-loss is almost always hormonal in origin. In cats hormonal skin disease is so rare as to be virtually non-existent. Hair loss is invariably caused by excessive self-grooming due to a generalised feeling of itchiness.

There may be a genetic component, and in most instances it can be very difficult to find a specific cause.

Prevention and treatment

Cats hospitalized in an insect-free environment have rapidly improved with no other treatment. In a home environment, flea and other insect control together with a hypoallergenic diet are preventative measures. Affected cats may need antibiotics and antihistamines, but most of all

Below left *Remember, if you only treat your cat, and not your home, the cat flea will take its meal from its second best source: you.*

Below right *This eosinophilic granuloma has been triggered by an allergic reaction to either flea saliva, food, or environmental allergens.*

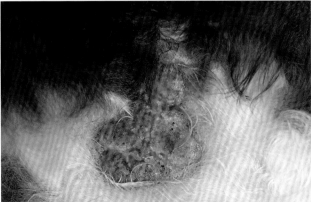

Cats are natural heat-seekers, but pale cats are more susceptible to skin cancer than their darker relatives. In sunny climates, control your cat's exposure to sunlight.

SOLAR DERMATITIS AND SKIN TUMOURS

Sun worshipping cats with white non-pigmented areas of skin can suffer serious skin inflammation (solar dermatitis), especially to the ears and nose. If the cat is not protected from the sun, a squamous cell carcinoma can develop. This is a malignant tumour which spreads locally, destroying the surrounding tissue.

Prevention and treatment
If skin damage is minor, keep your cat indoors during the sunniest part of the day. Some cats will tolerate sunblock (use SPF 30 or more), although most wash it off fairly quickly.
If the biopsy reveals a tumour is present, it should be surgically removed together with a margin around it to prevent recurrence. Removing ear flaps is fairly simple, although your cat's looks are rather drastically changed. Other treatments including radiotherapy are available at specialist centres. The prognosis is good if just the ears are affected and the damaged tissue is completely removed, but more guarded if not all of the affected tissue can be removed.

corticosteroids to suppress the over-reaction of the immune system. I also supplement a cat's diet with essential fatty acids (EFAs) containing a combination of evening primrose oil and fish oil.

Itchy skin has other causes
Effective topical flea-control products that kill fleas and prevent flea eggs from hatching have dramatically improved flea control, yet I still see lots of itchy cats.

Food intolerance or food allergy is perhaps the second most common cause of itchy skin. Pet food manufacturers have responded by producing an extensive variety of unique-protein or hypoallergenic diets.

The incidence of dust mite, fungal spore- and pollen allergies seems to have increased. Allergy testing in cats is less reliable than in dogs, although when I have identified offending airborne particles vaccine therapy has sometimes been dramatically effective.

Other skin parasites, such as ear mites and cheyletiella, can trigger an itchy skin response. Fortunately, these are killed by some of the topical treatments for fleas.

In the past it was assumed that cats are resistant to bacterial skin infections, but more recently there is evidence that some instances of itchy skin respond quickly to simple antibiotic treatment.

Ringworm is infectious
Ringworm is a fungal infection. The fungi feed on dead skin tissue and hair leaving round, hairless lesions usually on the face, ears, or paws. These are often reddened, scaly, and inflamed although they are not necessarily itchy (*see* page 138).

Ringworm is transmitted either by direct contact with another infected animal or through contact with fungal spores in carpets, bedding, or grooming equipment. Healthy adult cats have good resistance to ringworm but act as spore carriers; young cats and kittens are more susceptible, because their immune system hasn't fully developed.

Lesions are visible around ten to twelve days after exposure to spores, and a diagnosis is made by examining infected hairs with an ultraviolet light, microscope, and culture.

Prevention and treatment

It is as important to decontaminate the cat's environment as it is to treat affected cats with oral antifungal drugs and shampoos, because spores can survive for months. Bleach diluted at a ratio of 1:10 kills most spores. Steam cleaning carpets and furnishings is equally effective. Spores survive in vacuum cleaner bags and especially in bagless vacuum cleaners, which should be cleaned with diluted bleach. Wash all bedding in very hot water and confine your cat to one room during treatment and decontamination.

Fight wounds and abscesses

Skin abscesses, which are accumulations of pus, occur most frequently around the face or tail base and are often a result of puncture wounds inflicted during real or mock cat fights. The small puncture allows bacteria through the skin, and while the tiny wound heals quickly, the bacteria under the skin thrive and multiply.

Three to five days later a soft, painful swelling is felt. Infection into the bloodstream causes a fever, loss of appetite, lethargy, reluctance to play, and sensitivity to touch. If a leg is affected you may notice a limp. Abscesses are common wherever there are multiple cats.

Prevention and treatment

Neutering male cats is the most effective method for reducing the incidence and severity of fights. Keeping your cat inside at night will also reduce fighting opportunities. After a cat fight, inspect for tell-tale painful areas or puncture wounds, although punctures may be hard to find in thick hair. Concentrate your search around the head, neck, and forelegs and around the base of the spine, feeling for matted tufts of hair at puncture sites. Small holes are significant.

A ruptured abscess discharges thick, yellow, foul-smelling pus, and the more that discharges the better. Almost invariably a cat immediately feels healthier and may even resume eating. Remove hair from the wound and bathe away any discharge with warm, salty water or dilute hydrogen peroxide.

If the abscess does not rupture within a day or two, it is best to have it opened and drained by your vet. Antibiotic treatment given early to cats with bite wounds usually prevents abscesses and potentially expensive complications.

Ringworm can occur around the eyes and nose, making topical treatment more difficult. Washing your hands after handling a cat with ringworm prevents spread.

Eye, ear, and nose problems

Most conditions that affect the eyes, ears, and nose are easy to see. The eyes have visible damage or discharge, the ears are scratched or painful to touch, and either the nostrils have a discharge or your cat is sneezing more than normal. Most eye, nose, and ear conditions are caused by either infection, infestation, or trauma, but some are manifestations of allergy.

Ear mites are common

Ear mites, tiny spider-like white parasites, thrive in the cat's warm and humid ear canals, where they feed on debris and ear wax. Their presence causes inflammation and irritation, to which the body responds by producing more nutritious wax.

Cats scratch their ears or shake their head because of the itchiness. Some cats flatten their ears back or resent your touching the area; some cry out when scratching their ears. Inside the ear there is dark reddish brown or black debris and if you concentrate you can see moving white dots – the mites – in the sandy debris. If yeast and bacteria complicate the infestation, the discharge is smellier and more liquid.

Prevention and treatment

Some active ingredients in the spot-on treatments for fleas, such as selemectin, also kill ear mites both inside and outside the ear. When using one of the oily ear lotions, make sure the medicine is massaged daily and deeply into the cat's ear. Remove debris each day until none is left; this usually takes a week or more. Two weeks later treat again for a few days; this usually catches mites that have been on a short break and have now returned to the ear. Ear mites are very contagious to other cats and to dogs (but not to us), so check and treat all your pets.

Conjunctivitis caused by infection

Many cats have chronic red, swollen, watery or mucousy inflammation of the eye membranes, or "conjunctivitis". The flat facial conformation of the Persian predisposes it to tear overflow and conjunctivitis. Allergy will also cause watery conjunctivitis, but the most common causes are rhinotracheitis or herpes virus infections.

Many, if not most, cats are exposed to herpes virus as kittens and don't develop conjunctivitis, but herpes can lie dormant for years until given a chance when a cat's immune system is under stress. Then it becomes active, causing red, watery eyes. Opportunist bacteria infect the conjunctiva, and the discharge changes to yellow-green and sticky. An affected cat squints either from pain or to avoid light.

A direct stare can intimidate a cat, making it flinch away. Examine the eyes and conjunctiva from above, using your thumbs to gently expose the whites.

BRUCE'S HEAD-SHAKING TIP

Some cats shake their heads so intensely they rupture small blood vessels in the ear. A blood blister called a haematoma develops and this can sometimes fill the entire ear flap. If your cat has a hot, swollen ear, the haematoma needs attention but even more important, the cause of head shaking needs identification and treatment.

Prevention and treatment

The preventative vaccines against this virus, calicivirus (*see* page 135), and chlamydophila (*see* page 136) don't actually prevent infection, but they do dramatically reduce the severity of infectious conjunctivitis. Antibiotic eye ointment controls secondary infection, and kills chlamydophila outright.

I use pain control medication (meloxicam) and ask owners to cleanse the eyes three or four times daily with a homemade, room-temperature or warmer saline solution prepared with a quarter teaspoon of salt to a cup of water. Allergic conjunctivitis is more problematic, and needs treatment with antihistamines and anti-inflammatories.

Sneezing

The flu viruses (*see* page 135) and allergy account for most causes of sneezing. In both instances the discharge is clear and colourless. Sometimes the only evidence of discharge is the accumulation of small

amounts of dry, dark debris around the nostrils,which is easy to remove with damp cotton wool, even with a slight rub with your finger. If bacterial opportunists complicate the nasal inflammation or "rhinitis", the discharge becomes thicker, with a yellow-green appearance.

Sneezing and discharge from a single nostril usually suggests a foreign body in that side of the nose. In my experience, the most common is a blade of grass that, because of the texture of its surface, can only move in one direction, further in. Sneezing is the body's way of trying to discharge the foreign body.

Prevention and treatment

Once more, inoculation reduces the intensity of infectious causes of rhinitis (*see* pages 135–6). To control allergic rhinitis, identification and avoidance of the cause or use of antihistamines and anti-inflammatories may be needed.

Foreign bodies such as blades of grass usually need to be helped out under general anaesthesia by the vet. Sometimes I can gently tease the grass back out through the nostril, but on other occasions I need to use a scope and take it out through the nasopharynx, at the back of the mouth.

Top left *While many "spot-on" treatments kill ear mites, ear drops are beneficial for eliminating these parasites and other ear conditions. Approach from behind and beside, giving a treat immediately after.*

Top right *Flat-faced cats almost inevitably have impaired tear drainage into the nose. Colourless tears overflow and turn mahogany brown, staining the hair.*

Bottom left *The third eyelids may become visible, either because there is an eye problem or because there is a medical problem elsewhere in the body.*

Bottom right *Eye injuries are not uncommon, especially after combat. Fluorescein dye is applied to highlight any possible damage to the cornea.*

Mouth problems

Although a cat's breath is not naturally sweet smelling, foul breath almost always indicates a medical condition that needs immediate veterinary attention. Bad breath can be caused by kidney or liver disease, by feline leukemia, or by a viral infection. It may be caused by a foreign body, such as a piece of bone, stuck in the mouth, or even by an oral tumour in older cats, but overwhelmingly it is caused by tooth and gum disease. I anaesthetize more cats to treat their tooth and gum disease than for any other single reason.

Gums should be uniformly pink. If there are areas of red inflammation, especially around the roots of the teeth, the cat needs veterinary attention.

The progress of gum disease

Gingivitis is the early stage of gum disease, in which the gums become red and slightly swollen. Eventually they bleed easily.

If treatment is not received, gingivitis progresses to periodontal disease or periodontitis. This is more serious: bone is irreversibly lost, and so are teeth. Teeth become more brittle and break, and abscesses occur. An associated and common condition is "feline odontoclastic resorptive lesions", similar to cavities in us but not caused by the same bacteria (*see* below).

BRUCE'S TOOTH-CHECKING TIP

An easy way to check your cat's teeth and gums regularly is by running a cotton bud around the gum line. If you encounter blood or signs of pain, arrange for your vet to have a look.

Serious mouth problems almost always cause pain. Any of these signs warrant an immediate visit to the vet:
- Bad breath
- A reluctance to eat
- Food dropped from the mouth but then eaten
- Pawing at the face or mouth
- Drooling

Feline odontoclastic resorptive lesions (FORLs)

These are the most common dental problem found in cats. Two out of every three cats I see that are over six years old have FORLs. These lesions can occur on or just below the gum line and may affect only the root of a tooth. Sometimes they are obvious, with bright red gum growing up in an inverted V shape to cover them. Just as often they are below the gum line, evident only on X-ray or examination under general anaesthesia. FORLs cause pain, sometimes so intense that even

KIDNEY FAILURE AND LIVER DISEASE CAUSE BAD BREATH

Kidney and liver disease both lead to dental disease and cause bad breath. While treating primary gum disease (disease originating only in the gum) is very effective and makes a cat feel almost instantly better, secondary gum disease that appears as a consequence of other metabolic disease responds to treatment only if the primary condition, the kidney or liver condition, can be improved.

under general anaesthesia a cat may twitch when the tooth is probed! If your cat appears to want to eat but approaches its food hesitantly, assume until proven otherwise that it has mouth pain, and that pain may be caused by a FORL. Look in its mouth: you may notice a red line or redness and swelling where the tooth meets the gum.

FELINE STOMATITIS AND MOUTH TUMOURS

Cats can suffer from stomatitis, also known as lymphocytic plasmacytic syndrome (LPGS). This is an inflammation of the entire mouth caused by an allergic reaction to dental plaque. Signs include bad breath, weight loss, an inability to eat and drooling. Oral tumors also occur in cats. Both of these are serious conditions requiring dramatic interventions.

Prevention and treatment

Tartar build-up caused by plaque can be avoided either by cleaning your cat's teeth yourself or having your vet scale and polish them. There are specially formulated toothpastes and specially designed toothbrushes and finger brushes for cats. Avoid frothy human toothpaste.

Personally, I find it difficult to brush a cat's teeth, so I've let mine attend to their teeth and gums by eating bones. If you start them off as kittens, cats willingly eat bones. Yes, there are risks, but to me the risks from eating bones are less than the pain and risks associated with annual anaesthetics to scale and polish teeth. Special diets designed to reduce plaque formation are available and may be useful.

When veterinary attention is needed, extraction of the diseased tooth or teeth immediately alleviates pain. Even if a cat needs all of its teeth extracted, as happens with feline stomatitis, it adapts wonderfully well and can still eat most foods, including dry food.

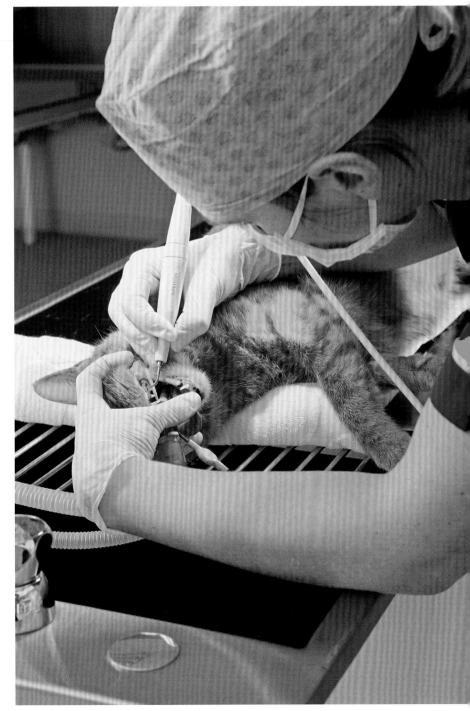

Scaling (scraping) away accumulated plaque and then polishing the teeth is the foundation of returning teeth and gums to good health.

Coughing cats

Chronic irritation to the airways is the most common cause of coughing in cats. It is variably called chronic bronchitis, allergic airway disease, allergic bronchitis, or asthma. Siamese cats appear to be particularly predisposed to this. But although this is the most common reason for coughing, there are others. The least serious is passing irritation from inhaled substances or foreign objects; more serious causes range from infections and infestations to trauma and some forms of heart disease. Persistent coughing should be checked by a vet to determine the cause and prevent it from progressing to serious breathing difficulties. And remember that cats don't just suffer allergies: they can cause them too.

What causes coughing

Coughing can be triggered by a cat inhaling irritants such as pollens or dust. It can also be triggered by cigarette smoke, even household cleaning sprays. What happens is the airways respond to the irritant by contraction of the smooth muscle that lines the bronchial tree, to prevent the irritant from moving deeper into the lung. Mucus is secreted to trap the irritant and a cough is triggered to expel it. All of these responses narrow the airways, which results in difficulty breathing.

Diseases such as bacterial infections, foreign bodies in the air passages, heart disease, or airway parasites can also cause similar clinical signs, but an asthmatic reaction is the most likely cause of coughing and wheezing.

Breathing is affected

While some cats gradually develop a chronic cough or wheeze, others suddenly find it very hard to breathe, especially to breathe out. They tuck themselves into a position they find easiest to breathe in, and the speed of breathing increases. Some cats are mildly affected. For others the condition is life threatening. In most instances, a simple X-ray reveals evidence of thickened small airways (bronchi) with air trapped in constricted areas, but this does not work in all cases. An examination with a bronchoscope may reveal excess mucus and reddening but, frustratingly, sometimes even bronchoscopy doesn't reveal visible abnormalities. If that is the case, your vet will take a wash from the airways, a bronchial lavage.

Prevention and treatment

While you and your vet try to determine what triggers asthma and eliminate it, the constricted air

At first glance this cat seems to be coughing, but its hunched stance means it is more likely to be regurgitating a hairball.

An inhaler or "puffer", designed for humans, is inserted into an adapter for a cat's face, and the canister is compressed. The cat breathes in its medication.

- Use a vacuum cleaner equipped with a HEPA filter to reduce dander in your carpets and soft furnishings without recycling it into the air.
- Have your cat neutered or spayed, because unneutered male cats produce more allergens than female cats, and neutering reduces sebum production.
- Have someone else groom your cat if possible, and sponge clean its coat daily to remove saliva.
- Get veterinary treatment for all skin and mouth conditions as soon as possible to reduce antigen production by your cat.
- Keep your home well ventilated, especially the area the litter tray is in.

passages are treated with a variety of drugs including anti-inflammatories, bronchodilators, and drugs to break down mucus (mucolytics). I also advise changing the litter to a low-dust type, avoiding all household sprays, and keeping cats indoors if asthma attacks occur after going outside.

The best way to give an asthmatic cat anti-inflammatory drugs (corticosteroids) is through an inhaler specially designed for cats (for an example, look for the Aerokat), which is tolerated surprisingly well. I think it's easier to use than giving tablets, and it targets the drug exactly where it's needed, in the air passages.

The prognosis for asthma depends on the severity of the disease and on the time delay before treatment is started. If asthma is allowed to become chronic, it can cause irreversible narrowing to the airways, which doesn't respond to drugs.

Are you allergic to cats?

Those of us who are allergic to cats, including me, react to a protein (called Fel D1) that is present not just in their dander, but also in their saliva. Occasionally I suffer from itchy eyes, sniffles, and a mild cough, but some Siamese and Burmese cats – and only in summer – trigger a proper asthmatic reaction in my chest. Reduce problems by reducing both the production of dander and your exposure to it.

- Use flea control products religiously, because a scratching cat throws more dander into the air.
- Don't let your cat into your bedroom, because dander accumulates wherever your cat lies.
- When possible allow your cat outdoors, because more dander will be left there.
- Avoid wearing wool clothing: wool acts like a magnet to allergens.

An allergy to cats need not be a bar to owning them; some breeders with several cats at home are allergic. Just take a little more care in day-to-day routines.

Gastrointestinal conditions

Problems affecting the stomach and intestines – and that means primarily vomiting, diarrhoea, and constipation – vie with skin problems as the most common reason people bring their cats to the vet. In many or even most instances, especially in young cats, the cause is banal, usually in the diet. But frustratingly, a cat can have the same clinical signs because of a very serious condition. For example, unexpected vomiting is likely to be caused by something irritating the stomach wall; that's easy to treat with diet change and medicines that protect the wall. But, as all vets have experienced, it can be caused by a cancer developing in the stomach wall. Good diagnostics are vital for treating gastrointestinal conditions.

Above *With young cats such as this one, a little trial and error is needed to find the diet that is ideal for its individual gastrointestinal system.*

Below *Cats can be noisy when they vomit. This can be caused by something as simple as eating grass, but also by serious medical conditions.*

Vomiting

Cats naturally vomit occasionally, but if they continue to eat, play, pee, and poop normally, it's more a mess for you than a cause for concern.

But if your cat vomits habitually or persistently, even if it seems otherwise perfectly well, there may be a significant medical reason. If your cat has other medical signs, especially lethargy, there is definite cause for concern and medical treatment is urgently needed.

Vomiting is not an illness. It's a clinical sign that something is amiss. Reasons for vomiting include:

- Eating or diet problems
- Hairballs
- Medicines, including worming medicines
- Poisons, whether licked, eaten, or absorbed through the skin
- Heat stroke
- Motion sickness
- Intestinal problems, including irritations, inflammations, constipation, obstructions, ulcerations, irritable bowel syndrome, and intestinal worms
- Metabolic diseases, including diabetes, hyperthyroidism, kidney disease, liver disease, and pancreatic disease
- Infections, including gastrointestinal infections, womb infection (pyometra), and abscess infections
- Various cancers
- Urinary tract conditions, including infections, obstructions, lower urinary tract diseases, and kidney failure

Eating and vomiting problems

In young cats, most instances of vomiting that I see are caused either by what is eaten or by the way a cat eats. Food intolerance, especially to protein, also seems to have increased during the time

I've been in practice. Other causes of vomiting include a too-rapid change in diet, eating too quickly or overeating, eating houseplants, or (less commonly) eating food that has gone off or taking prey such as small mammals, lizards, or other material.

Prevention and treatment
Trial and error is the only way to overcome vomiting caused by food intolerance. As a general rule, I gradually switch cats that are on chicken-, beef-, or lamb-based diets over to fish-based foods. If this isn't effective, I use a diet where the protein has been hydrolyzed into its component amino acids (*see* page 78).

Cats that eat too quickly are treated by leaving small portions of food in paper bags throughout the house, which forces the cat to work to find small amounts and eat them gradually.

Hairballs
A cat's stomach and intestines are designed to handle hair, but some cats – and not just longhaired ones – accumulate hair in the stomach. Rather than passing through the intestines, it gets regurgitated back, usually exactly where you step out of bed in the morning. An occasional hairball is normal, but frequent regurgitation needs attention.

Prevention and treatment
Prevent excess hair from being swallowed through combing the coat frequently. Brushing isn't effective; a bristle brush just doesn't remove enough dead hair, especially down. Use a fine-toothed comb

Rodents are a natural diet, but if a rodent killed by (or dying from) rodenticide is eaten by a cat, that cat may be affected by the poison.

on shorthaired cats and a wider-toothed comb on those with longer hair.

Many cats "self-medicate" by eating grass or plants. Coarse plant fibre helps them regurgitate hairballs, but remember, many cats without hairballs also eat plant fibre simply because they're attracted to it.

Treat hairballs with a proprietary hairball treatment. These usually contain either petroleum jelly or mineral oil. You can also feed a commercial hairball diet, which is higher in fibre than regular cat food. Fibre, usually in the form of beet pulp or powdered cellulose, helps to sluice hair through the intestines. Take care if you are adding fibre to a regular diet: too much fibre may cause either diarrhoea (because it absorbs moisture) or constipation (because it is bulky). As with any dietary change, make the switch gradually and monitor the litter tray carefully for the results.

Diarrhoea

Cat poop is normally well formed, quite smelly (because there is so much protein in the diet), and consistent in colour, usually brown. It's usually dumped following a set routine or pattern.

Any change in that routine – change in colour or consistency, or the appearance of blood or mucus – may be important. Diarrhoea varies from merely a soft consistency, through watery, to explosive watery-to-bloody. Like vomiting, diarrhoea is not an illness, but a symptom. Causes of diarrhoea include:

- Diet problems, including dietary intolerances
- Medicines
- Poisons, whether licked, eaten, or absorbed through the skin
- Intestinal problems, including inflammatory bowel disease, intestinal worms, and tumours
- Intestinal infections caused by viruses, bacteria, and single-celled parasites such as giardia
- Metabolic diseases, including diabetes, hyperthyroidism, kidney disease, liver disease, and pancreatic disease
- Infections, including gastrointestinal infections, womb infection (pyometra), and abscess infections

Causes and signs

Forms of diarrhoea vary. Diarrhoea that is caused by problems in the small intestine is often watery and copious, and cats quickly lose weight. In large bowel diarrhoea, cats pass frequent but smaller amounts of soft poop, sometimes containing fresh blood or mucus.

In cats that go outside, or in a multi-cat household, it can be difficult to know what's happening. With severe diarrhoea, even outdoor cats may have accidents in the house because they cannot get outside in time. Remains of poop stuck to the fur under the tail is an obvious clue, and watch for vomiting too, because this often accompanies diarrhoea. Some cats with diarrhoea drink more.

Prevention and treatment

Avoid any sudden change in diet: this is, in my experience, the most common cause of diarrhoea. If your cat has sudden

BRUCE'S SAMPLE TIP

When taking your cat to the vet for treatment for diarrhoea, take a recent stool sample with you. It can be checked for giardia, an underdiagnosed cause of chronic diarrhoea, as well as for worms, undigested food matter, and (if warranted) for bacteria.

diarrhoea but is otherwise bright, simply withhold food for a day then return to the diet that previously produced well-formed stools. Some cats develop lactose intolerance; for these, avoid dairy products. Inquisitive kittens and cats may eat things they shouldn't, so cover your kitchen waste.

Alternatively, feed a bland, highly digestible, low-fat diet, such as chicken with baby-cereal rice. Give this as three or four small meals a day to reduce the load on the intestine. The diet can then be gradually changed back to the cat's normal food over the next two to three days. If diarrhoea was caused by scavenging, it usually corrects itself.

Recent research shows that even with self-limiting diarrhoea, the condition clears up a day faster if you add an appropriate "probiotic" supplement to the diet, so these are worth trying.

BRUCE'S ANTIBIOTIC TIP

Cat owners often ask if I will use antibiotics to treat their cat's diarrhoea, but antibiotics are only useful if a specific bacterial cause is found in faecal cultures or if the intestines are severely damaged. In most instances of diarrhoea, antibiotics are not helpful, and they can even make the problem worse.

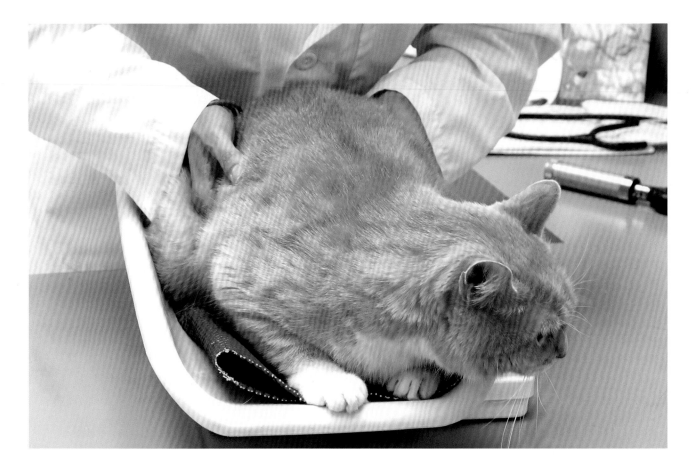

Prevention and treatment of infections and infestations

Parvovirus (panleukopenia), coronavirus, and rotavirus infections are common viral causes of diarrhoea. Salmonella and campylobacter are two bacteria that can cause diarrhoea. Infestations of roundworms, hookworms, and protozoa such as giardia can all cause diarrhoea. Many of these causes can be avoided through appropriate vaccination and worming (*see pages 134–41*).

Treatment for diarrhoea caused by infection or infestation is tailored to the individual circumstances and the seriousness of the condition. Antibiotics and intravenous fluids are often required. In very severe or long-standing diarrhoea,

your vet will carry out tests to determine the cause and then the most appropriate treatment for it.

Treatment of inflammatory bowel disease

There can be a trial and error stage in the treatment of inflammatory bowel disease. Because there are so many trigger factors, treatment must be developed on an individual basis, and diet always plays an important role.

I usually feed a diet sourced from a protein that the cat has not eaten in the past six months, for example venison, duck, or deep sea fish. A cat needs to be kept on this diet for at least six weeks to judge whether it is beneficial.

Weight monitoring is important in all gastrointestinal disease. Weight loss is of vital significance, although weight gain can also be of clinical importance.

Additional drugs to control inflammation to the intestines and accompanying diarrhoea are usually needed.

Constipation

Chronic constipation is a common condition, especially in older cats. A constipated cat passes stools less frequently, with difficulty, or not at all. Constipated cats often show signs of pain when trying to pass poop. Affected cats make increased trips to the litter tray and spend longer time on it. You see non-productive straining and it can be difficult to decide whether your cat is trying to urinate or defecate. In some instances a cat passes fluid around the impacted stool in the colon. This happens when the retained faeces irritates the lining of the large intestine and stimulates fluid secretion, and it can be mistaken for diarrhoea. Constipated cats often lose their appetite and vomit as the condition progresses.

Causes of constipation

Reluctance to defecate can be for behavioural reasons, such as a dirty tray or competition from other cats. Any medical reason, such as pain when defecating, can also make a cat reluctant to use the litter tray.

Cats that are dehydrated reabsorb more fluid from the colon. As a result the stool becomes hard and dry. Chronic renal failure is a common cause of dehydration.

Injuries can damage either the nerves that control contraction of the bowels or the pelvic canal through which the colon passes, and either of these forms of injury can cause constipation. Other injuries can cause just the opposite, a lack of sphincter muscle control and consequent faecal incontinence.

A stricture is caused either by scar tissue in the bowel wall from a previous injury or by some types of tumour that can infiltrate the bowel wall. Other obstructions can block the colon: for example, matter such as hair, foreign material, or bone lodged in the large intestine can obstruct it.

In idiopathic megacolon, the smooth muscle that normally contracts to propel the faeces towards the rectum loses its ability to do so. Although the cause is not known, this is, in my experience, the most common cause of constipation in older cats.

Prevention and treatment

Chronic constipation is a very common problem especially in older cats. Early and uncomplicated constipation usually responds to changes in the diet and lubricant laxatives.

Laxatives loosen bowel contents to allow stool to pass through the colon. Some act as lubricants (similar to hairball treatments) while others stimulate the colon to greater activity (*see* panel opposite for greater detail). Cats should be well hydrated before being given laxatives, because most of them lead to water retention in the colon.

Mild constipation may be relieved with just a small lubricant laxative. In more severely affected cats, I need to give a cat a warm water enema, usually under general anaesthesia, combined with manual evacuation.

More chronic or complicated constipation is harder to control, takes dedication on the part of the owner and

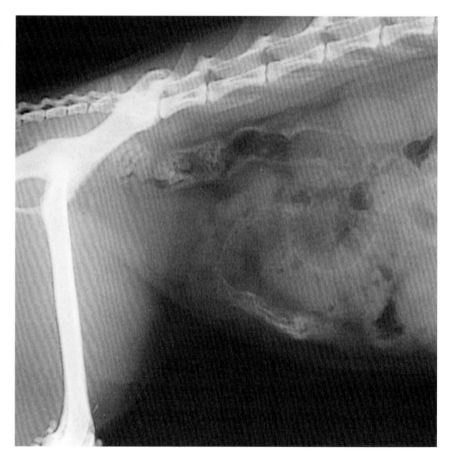

This cat needs urgent treatment for its constipation: the X-ray shows large intestines overfilled with faeces together with some gas (the dark areas).

may require surgery to improve, although surgery is not always a cure.

If constipation is a result of dehydration, an intravenous drip is often needed to overcome the primary cause. At home, a cat's hydration can be improved by switching from dried kibbles to wet food and by adding water to the food. To treat chronic dehydration, I show willing cat owners how they can give daily subcutaneous fluids.

Megacolon

Retained stool in a constipated cat eventually distends the colon; if this happens, even for only a few days, the colon's nerves and muscles can both become damaged, sometimes permanently. This creates a condition called megacolon, which is harder to treat than simple constipation.

Prokinetic drugs improve neuromuscular transmission and are useful in mild to moderate cases of megacolon. None are licenced for use in cats, so they can only be given with informed consent.

Surgery to remove the permanently damaged portion of the colon is sometimes needed.

Poisons

Cats are fussy eaters, so they actively choose to eat poisonous substances less frequently than dogs do. On the other hand they are fastidiously clean, so are more likely to consume poisons that contaminate their hair.

Of all cats, those that are young, inquisitive, or just plain bored are most likely to eat hazardous things. Tender household plants or cut flowers pose the greatest risk and because they are so fashionable, Easter lilies and other lilies are now a common cause of poisoning. Eating just one leaf of these can result in severe vomiting and listlessness within two hours.

As an added complication, the livers of cats also lack certain enzymes that help to break down poisons. As a result of this, common chemicals, including drugs that are safe for us or for dogs, are potentially lethal to cats. When cats do become poisoned they are less likely to recover than dogs.

Avoid poisonous plants

Take an inventory of all your indoor plants and flowers, check them against lists of toxic plants (*see* panel below for guidance) and flowers and discard the dangerous ones. Cats enjoy nibbling on vegetation, so supply grass to chew on. If you know your cat has eaten a poisonous plant or flower, get immediate veterinary attention.

Antifreeze kills cats

Ethylene glycol is sometimes added to water in fountains to prevent freezing, and cats love to drink flowing water! Ethylene glycol is naturally sweet, so antifreeze often contains a "bittering" agent, but at low concentrations this may not deter a cat. Antifreeze also easily contaminates the feet or hair if it leaks from a car radiator onto the ground, and under a car is a warm place for a cat to rest in cold weather.

Like so many other poisons, this one causes vomiting and listlessness followed by a loss of balance, all within 12 hours. Cats require immediate and intensive treatment to manage their kidney failure.

Left *Fastidious feline grooming virtually guarantees that any toxic substance on the coat will be ingested. It may also be absorbed directly though the skin.*

Right *Water can be contaminated with chemicals or parasites; provide enough clean water at home and your cat may not pick up the habit of drinking elsewhere.*

CLEAN A CONTAMINATED COAT

Remove as much contamination as possible by clipping off any affected hair, then wash the cat in warm, soapy water. Thoroughly towel dry. Oily material can be removed by rubbing with clean, warm cooking oil, then wiping it all off. If you think the cat may have ingested any of the substance already, take it to your vet as soon as possible.

Dangerous drugs

We unwittingly poison cats, sometimes even kill them, by trying to make them feel better or to prevent them from getting fleas. Some common painkiller drugs, safe for us, can kill cats, as can some pesticides and household cleaners.

Painkillers

Paracetamol can kill a cat at as little as 45mg per 1kg (2lb) of body weight: that's just one of our tablets for a normal-sized cat. The poisoned cat may drool, vomit, and appear depressed; it can die in less than 24 hours.

Just 25mg of aspirin per 1kg (2lb) of body weight can cause acute poisoning: that's *less* than a single aspirin tablet for a normal-sized cat. The poisoned cat may vomit, appear depressed, go off its food, and rapidly develop kidney failure. Even lower doses than this, if given frequently, can cause stomach ulcers or liver disease.

Around 50mg of ibuprofen per 1kg (2lb) of body weight is toxic to cats. Once more, this is less than a single maximum-strength human tablet. Ibuprofen also causes vomiting, lethargy, and blood in vomit or the stool.

Flea treatments

Permethrin is a common insecticide found in many over-the-counter flea treatments for dogs, but it is highly toxic to cats. Only use flea treatments that state they are for cats. Permethrin is one of the most common causes of avoidable poisoning in cats: one in five die.

Insect repellents

Used by us on our clothing to ward off mosquitoes and other biting insects, DEET is toxic if licked by cats. Signs of poisoning include skin irritation, vomiting, tremors, and excitation; loss of coordination, even seizures.

Household products

Many common household disinfectants and decking or path cleaners contain phenols: they are the ones that turn cloudy when they are mixed with water. Cats absorb phenol through the skin or ingest them by licking their paws after walking on surfaces recently treated with these products.

BRUCE'S POISONING TIP — GET VETERINARY ATTENTION

Don't try to make your cat sick by giving washing soda or salt. These don't work well in cats. Let your vet know you are on your way and if you know what has been swallowed, take the package with you. Wrap your cat for the journey. This will prevent it from hurting itself or you and also prevents it from licking itself further if there is a poisonous substance on its coat.

Problems urinating

Feline lower urinary tract disorders (FLUTD) are less common than they were 30 years ago. Today, less than 3 per cent of cats suffer from FLUTD, but it's a painful problem for those affected. FLUTD is typically first seen in overweight, indoor, neutered, two- to seven-year-old cats that take little exercise and eat dry food. Persian cats also appear to be more at risk. An affected cat may visit the litter tray frequently, strain to urinate, pass very small amounts at a time, lick its genitals more frequently, or have blood in the urine. Some cats associate their pain with the litter tray so they urinate in the bathtub or sink, or on your laundry or bed. Some male cats develop blockages and can't urinate at all. This is excruciatingly painful and requires urgent veterinary attention, day or night.

Variable causes

Bladder infection is an uncommon cause of FLUTD. Of cats under ten years of age with the condition, less than 2 per cent have an infection.

Just under 15 per cent of affected cats have bladder stones, half of which are struvite, and half calcium oxalate. These are what can block the urethra in male cats. Struvite, or "triple-phosphate" stones were more common in the 1970s and 1980s. Calcium oxalate crystals were once rare, but their incidence increased when highly acidified struvite-treatment diets became available. Struvite crystals can be dissolved by diet, although this can take a long time; calcium oxalate crystals can't.

And the rest? Most cats with FLUTD, about two out of three, have what is called "idiopathic cystitis", which unfortunately means "bladder inflammation of unknown cause".

A possible cause

Nerves within the bladder wall are stimulated by bladder inflammation. This may be caused by stones, crystals, bacteria, or tumours, but also by the brain in response to stress. Regardless of how these nerves are stimulated, they release certain chemicals that increase local pain and inflammation.

BRUCE'S ANTIDEPRESSANT TIP

Antidepressants such as amitriptyline are used to treat interstitial cystitis in people and have been used, sometimes effectively, for cats. It isn't known whether they work because they are antidepressants or because they are also painkillers and anti-inflammatories. There can be behavioural side effects.

Cats in the wild get most of the water they need from eating fresh prey, so domestic cats are not naturally inclined to drink a lot of water.

BRUCE'S CRANBERRY TIP

Cranberry extract is beneficial for dogs, which often have cystitis caused by bacterial bladder infection; it may prevent bacteria from attaching to the bladder wall. Because bacteria are not present in most cases of FLUTD, this extract is probably less beneficial for cats.

A thin layer of protective mucus called glycosaminoglycan (GAG) lines the bladder wall and helps prevent bacteria or crystals from sticking to it. Defects in this protective layer may allow noxious substances within the urine to cause inflammation. Some cats with idiopathic cystitis have reduced levels of GAG.

Medical treatment

Most instances of non-obstructive FLUTD are self-limiting, usually resolving within five to ten days, but the condition is very painful and distressing to the cat, so immediate treatment is almost always beneficial. While infection is a rare cause of FLUTD, some antibiotics – especially those in the penicillin family – also have anti-inflammatory or pain-relieving effects, so I use them.

For male cats that repeatedly develop life-threatening blockages, surgery to widen the urethra may be necessary.

Whether they work as pain killers, as anti-inflammatories, or in some other way, GAG supplements given by mouth or subcutaneous injection benefit some cats. In people there are differences in the effectiveness of different GAGs, and the same is likely to be true in cats.

Dietary changes

Diet is a component of FLUTD, though usually not the sole cause. Encourage your cat to increase its water intake. This is the single most important factor. Simply feed commercial or home-prepared wet food or thoroughly soaked dry food. Feed a dry food designed to increase water turnover only if your cat flatly refuses to eat anything else.

Take care with commercial diets. Avoid giving dry cat foods, particularly high-fibre or "light" ones, because they contribute to overall dehydration and high urine concentration. Use highly acidified diets only to dissolve properly diagnosed struvite stones, and give them for as short a time as possible.

Reduce stress

Cats that are predisposed to idiopathic cystitis have a greater than average level of arousal and response to stress. If they live indoors, they can't take control, for example by running away. Stress can trigger recurrences of idiopathic cystitis, so control multi-cat problems, keep the litter tray in a suitable location, and make any changes as smoothly as possible. If you can control the weather, that helps too! A Feliway plug-in (*see* page 121) may help to reduce anxiety.

Elderly cats

I find older cats irresistible. When I try to analyze why I admire these grey-eyed, stiff-jointed oldies, I think it's because they are more sociable, more affectionate, more demanding, and yes, more needy. Older cats often become more dependent on us. They want more of us. Stoics that they are however, they never complain, even when they're feeling terrible. In the United States, Canada, Germany, the United Kingdom and undoubtedly elsewhere, cats over ten years of age make up one third or more of the owned population. Where I practise, those over ten years old make up over half of all the cats I see.

Old age is not an illness

I'm routinely asked, when I examine an older cat that has "slowed down" whether it is " simply old age". My answer is that it isn't old age but rather a specific medical condition, or as often happens, several conditions, that just occur more frequently in old age. These include arthritis – perhaps the most under-recognized condition in elderly cats – chronic kidney disease, heart disease, overactive thyroid glands, cancers, and true senility.

Many other medical conditions also occur more frequently in old age, including diabetes (*see* pages 150–1), tooth and gum disease (*see* pages 158–9), lower urinary tract problems (*see* pages 170–1), and gastrointestinal and liver disease (*see* pages 162–7). Whatever the medical condition, caring for an older cat is like looking after a cross between a little child and an elderly relative.

Arthritis is common

As a veterinary student I was taught that cats, because we haven't tampered with their form and structure too much, have the good fortune to develop arthritis only in joints that were previously injured or damaged. That was hopelessly wrong. Studies looking at radiographs of older cats revealed that 90 per cent of cats over 12 had evidence of degenerative joint disease! Osteoarthritis is extremely common in older cats. It is seriously under-diagnosed.

Osteoarthritis

Osteoarthritis is a type of arthritis in which the normal cartilage that cushions the joint gradually wears away with time, exposing underlying bone that becomes inflamed and painful. Some breeds are more predisposed to develop arthritis in specific joints – for example hip dysplasia in Maine Coons, and knee arthritis in Abyssinians. Scottish Folds are particularly prone to arthritis in many joints, while Burmese cats develop elbow arthritis more than other breeds. Being overweight does not cause arthritis; it does however make it worse, and since the vast majority of cats eventually develop arthritis, excess weight is a major cause of needless pain.

Watch your cat carefully

It's easier to spot joint discomfort in dogs than in cats. Rather than limp but still play, as dogs do, cats hide their discomfort. If a joint hurts, they reduce physical activity, and this passive behaviour efficiently disguises their pain. If your cat exhibits any of these changes, it may have joint pain:
- Hesitation when jumping up or down from furniture
- Unwillingness to jump up or down from furniture

Reduced physical activity and sleeping more are as likely to be caused by age-related discomfort as by advancing age alone, but discomfort is manageable.

- Reduced physical activity
- Going outside less or playing less
- Less hunting and exploring
- Excessively licking a specific joint
- Less grooming activity
- Matted hair, especially in areas that need body contortions to be groomed
- Sleeping in new and more accessible locations
- New and unexpected difficulties using the cat flap
- Missing the litter tray, especially if it has high sides
- Increased irritability, especially when petted or touched
- Reduced interest in or response to your petting
- Overgrown, even ingrowing claws

Although joint pain is so common in older cats, general pain and other medical conditions can also cause these passive behaviour changes.

Home care for the arthritic cat

Adjustments at home are easy and simple for improving your cat's quality of life. You vet will also provide medication and nutritional advice. Provide soft, comfortable beds in accessible, warm, and quiet places. Cats often enjoy the feeling of security of enclosed places, so consider an "igloo" bed. Microwaveable warmers are available to make beds cosier, but use electrical heating pads only if you can carefully monitor them. Cats love radiator hammocks, but these can be problematic for the arthritic cat, who may benefit from steps to get in and out of it.

Provide either carpeted steps or a carpeted ramp to help your cat get to higher places such as your sofa or bed, if it sleeps there. If the cat flap is high, provide a ramp there too and fix the flap open so there's no need to push through.

Provide an indoor litter tray, even if your cat has always used the outdoors, and make sure it has low sides. Arthritic cats sometimes feel more comfortable on softer varieties of litter. Keep the litter tray, food, and water bowls all on the same floor. This is one circumstance where it may even be useful to have them relatively close to each other.

Gently groom your cat more, especially the areas that are more difficult for it to reach, such as the bum. Check the claws routinely. It's common in my experience for the claws of cats with arthritis to become overgrown, sometimes to such an extent that they puncture the pads and make walking even more painful.

Diet and medication

Use any of the good-quality nutritional joint supplements specifically formulated for cats. These usually contain essential fatty acids (EFAs) to reduce inflammation, natural glucosamine and chondroitin to help improve cartilage quality, and anti-oxidants to reduce free-radical damage. The therapeutic value of joint nutrients has not been studied

An elderly cat may be less sleek because it is grooming less due to discomfort associated with arthritis. This can be treated with diet supplements and medication.

in cats, but they have been shown to be effective in dogs, horses, and people. They may help in early or mild osteoarthritis but not on their own, alone, in more advanced joint disease.

Most cats with arthritis are over 12 years old, so other medical conditions such as kidney or thyroid problems may also be present. The non-steroid anti-inflammatory drug meloxicam is very effective for reducing pain, but must be used with caution or even avoided when there are additional problems such as dehydration, low blood pressure, vomiting, diarrhoea, or kidney or liver problems. Increased water consumption is good for all older cats but especially for those being given meloxicam. Consider switching to wet foods or providing an attractive water fountain.

Finally, I still don't know what to think about acupuncture. If a cat hates visiting the vet, avoid it. If a cat hates strangers, avoid it. If a cat hates needles, avoid it. And that's probably the majority of cats. But I have a veterinary acupuncturist colleague who does treat occasional individuals, and it seems to be useful when used very selectively.

BRUCE'S WEIGHT-CONTROL TIP

With your vet's help, decide on a weight target for your cat to achieve over a six-to nine-month period. Overweight cats should lose weight slowly. Too-rapid weight loss can result in serious metabolic problems, such as hepatic lipidosis, in which fat accumulates to dangerously high levels in their liver.

Chronic kidney failure

Chronic kidney failure occurs when the kidneys gradually lose their ability to filter and remove waste products from the blood. In younger cats there are specific causes such as infections, toxic damage, or immune system problems, but for most elderly cats the cause of chronic kidney failure is unknown. One in five cats over 15 years of age has chronic kidney failure, making it three times more common in cats than it is in dogs. Between two-thirds and three-quarters of all kidney tissue has been destroyed before visible signs of kidney failure develop.

Watch for these changes

The signs of kidney failure are both gradual and vague: some weight loss, less interest in food, increased thirst, more urine passed, a little lethargy, and a dull coat. If these are left undiagnosed and untreated, the signs become more dramatic: dehydration, depression, vomiting, foul-smelling breath, mouth ulcers, and even convulsions.

All of these changes can also be caused by other diseases, so an accurate diagnosis is made by analyzing blood and urine samples for urea and creatinine, two substances normally excreted by the kidneys. Cats with kidney failure may also have high blood pressure and be anaemic.

Bruce's testing tip

Remember, by the time any visible signs develop, a cat has already irreversibly lost most of its kidney tissue. Annual preventative blood sampling in cats over ten years old picks up the blood changes of early kidney disease long before the condition becomes clinical.

Vital diet changes

Many of the toxic products that accumulate in the blood with kidney failure are a result of protein breakdown, so feed a low-protein diet. Too little protein in the diet, however, can lead to excessive weight loss, which is detrimental to general health, so specially formulated commercial "kidney" or "renal" diets are preferable to home cooking. These diets are also low in phosphate, so are good for protecting the kidneys from further damage, and contain added and potentially beneficial fibre and unsaturated fatty acids.

If your cat finds all low-protein diets unpalatable, even when warmed or mixed with normal food, give normal cat food. Eating regular food is better than eating too little food. Your vet can supply you with a phosphate "binder" to reduce the amount of absorbed phosphate.

Home and veterinary care

Because the kidneys have lost some of their ability to concentrate urine and conserve water, cats with chronic kidney failure are more likely to become dehydrated. Maintain good fluid intake by feeding tinned or sachet foods rather than dry foods. Offer water from several different bowls. Try a "pet fountain". Chicken- and tuna-flavoured waters are commercially available for them.

High blood pressure is associated with chronic kidney failure and can cause sudden bleeding into the eyes or retinal detachment, both of which cause blindness. Bleeding into the brain can cause neurological changes. ACE-inhibitors, such as benazepril, reduce blood pressure and can be beneficial to some cats with kidney failure. Cats with advanced kidney failure often benefit from intermittent fluids either by intravenous drip or by injection.

The rate of deterioration in chronic kidney failure varies markedly between individuals. Diet changes that are started when a blood sample shows increased waste products but before a cat is seen to be drinking more probably prolong the cat's life expectancy by on average around 18 months.

Anaemia is serious

Anaemia is a serious condition. It is not a disease in itself, but rather the consequence of a specific condition. If your cat's gums look pale it may be anaemic. Cats with severe anaemia are more lethargic than normal, breathe faster, and have a faster heart rate. Some anaemic cats lick bricks or concrete, or eat cat litter or soil. Others are jaundiced, their gums and eyes taking on a yellow tinge. Anaemia develops either if there is a loss of blood (haemorrhage), for example from internal bleeding from accidents, tumours, or disease, or because red blood cells simply disintegrate (haemolysis). A range of infections, drugs, tumours, and disease can cause haemolysis. The kidneys produce a hormone called erythropoietin, which stimulates red blood cell production in the bone marrow. Any condition that suppresses production in the bone marrow, including chronic kidney disease, can lead to a form of anaemia where no new red blood cells are produced. Mild anaemia is not significant, but more serious anaemia causes lethargy and weakness. For cats with advanced kidney disease, your vet may use anabolic steroids, iron supplements, or synthetic erythropoietin to overcome anaemia. Synthetic erythropoietin only buys a window of improvement. The body soon learns to reject it as "foreign".

Heart disease

Cardiomyopathy, which means disease of the heart muscle, is often not diagnosed until something dramatic happens – such as sudden blindness because of associated high blood pressure, acute hind leg pain because of blood clots, or breathing difficulties because fluid builds up in or around the heart.

Two types of cardiomyopathy occur. A cat with thickening of its heart muscle, called hypertrophic cardiomyopathy (HCM), has less space in its heart chambers for blood, so it pumps less with each contraction. In other cats the heart muscle becomes scarred (fibrotic) and loses its ability to expand and contract as it once did. This is called restrictive cardiomyopathy (RCM). Different drugs are used to treat the different forms of heart muscle disease.

Heart failure is sudden

By the time I see a cat with loss of appetite, breathlessness, and lethargy, its long-standing heart disease has reached a crisis. These clinical signs appear typically over a few hours or a day.

DILATED CARDIOMYOPATHY AND DIET

Thirty years ago, some cat food makers failed to put enough taurine (which is destroyed by cooking) in their foods. The resulting dietary deficiency caused a virtual epidemic of dilated cardiomyopathy (DCM). In this, the heart's chambers, rather than thickening as in HCM, become dilated and weakened to such an extent the heart is no longer able to pump sufficient blood to meet the body's demand. DCM is now rare, but it can still occur in any cat that is fed a taurine-deficient diet.

BRUCE'S GENETIC TESTING TIP

Genetic tests for hypertrophic cardiomyopathy (HCM) are available for particular mutations found in roughly 30 per cent of tested Maine Coons and Ragdolls. A positive test result means that that cat is genetically predisposed to HCM. A negative test only means that the cat does not have that one particular mutation known to cause HCM.

The inefficient heart is no longer able to meet the demands for pumping blood around the body. Fluid leaks into or around the lungs, preventing them from functioning normally; that's what causes breathlessness. Unlike dogs, coughing is not a major sign of heart failure in cats. Cardiomyopathy also occurs in young, middle aged, and especially male cats. Genetic mutations that can lead to HCM have been identified in the Maine Coon and Ragdoll breeds.

A possible dramatic complication of cardiomyopathy is that blood sits for longer in the heart and clots. Bits of this large clot break off, are pumped through the circulation, and become trapped in smaller arteries, most often where the blood supply to the hind legs and tail divides into three arteries. The resulting obstruction causes sudden excruciating pain and loss of the use the hind legs and tail. Owners may think their cat has been hit by a car and has a broken spine. With immediate treatment, some cats recover the use of their limbs, but the long term outlook is often terribly bleak.

Diagnosis and treatment

A definitive diagnosis is made using X-rays, ECG and ultrasound examination (echocardiography), and treatment varies

HIGH BLOOD PRESSURE

High blood pressure, also called hypertension, is common in older cats and can damage blood vessels. The retinas of the eye are particularly sensitive to hypertensive damage. Affected cats appear confused and disorientated, with widely dilated pupils. Retinal detachment is an emergency situation, as blindness will become permanent unless the retina re-attaches within a few days. Hypertension also damages the kidneys, the heart (causing a thickening of the walls as the muscle has to work harder pumping against high resistance within the blood vessels), and the brain, where it causes small blood vessels to rupture. Drugs that lower blood pressure are used. Unlike in us, primary hypertension is rare in cats. There is almost always a specific cause or causes, such as hyperthyroidism and chronic kidney disease, and these need attention for treatment to be effective.

with the initial signs, severity, and type of cardiomyopathy. If an underlying cause such as an overactive thyroid is identified and corrected, the cardiac condition may improve. Where no underlying cause is found, treatment is aimed at management of heart rate and hypertension symptoms. Cardiomyopathies are usually progressive, although progression is sometimes wonderfully slow.

If fluid has accumulated in the lungs, diuretics are used to reduce circulating volume. Fluid around the lungs (pleural effusion) is usually removed directly via a needle or catheter through the chest wall. ACE inhibitors are used to reduce

Cats are understated about their health. Elderly cats may appear completely normal until high blood pressure suddenly causes a devastating incident.

High blood pressure caused this cat to lose its sight suddenly. Blood pressure should be monitored at least twice yearly from 12 years of age.

the heart's work load, while calcium channel blockers help the heart muscle relax, so there is more room for blood to fill the chambers. While aspirin is very toxic to cats, it is often used in low doses, twice weekly, to reduce the risk from blood clots. Except in cases where taurine deficiency is suspected, no specific dietary change is needed, although overweight cats benefit from weight loss.

The outlook

The response to treatment depends on the type and severity of the disease, whether congestive heart failure (where the heart cannot pump enough blood to the body) has developed, and whether heart disease is primary or secondary to another condition such as hypertension or hyperthyroidism. Some cases remain stable for years, but cats that produce blood clots have the gravest prognosis.

MANAGING BLINDNESS

A detached retina as a result of high blood pressure is a common cause of sudden blindness in older cats. Whatever causes blindness, other senses partly compensate. Cats continue to navigate using sound, vibration, and their magnificent long sensory facial whiskers, the vibrissae. These act like radar. If your cat is blind, stick to a routine and whenever possible avoid moving any furniture around. Continue to play using squeaky toys close enough for your blind cat to bat or bite, and introduce new objects or odours gradually. If you have several cats, don't let any of the others chew your blind cat's whiskers!

Overactive thyroid gland

Hyperthyroidism is a very common disease in older cats, caused by an increase in production of thyroid hormones from enlarged thyroid glands in the cat's neck. In most cases this is caused by a benign tumour called an adenoma, but the underlying cause of this change is still unknown.

Thyroid hormones help control the body's metabolic rate, so cats with hyperthyroidism burn up energy and lose weight despite eating very well. While both thyroid glands are usually involved, one gland may be more severely affected than the other. Cats respond extremely well to treatment, and the outlook is very good if the condition is diagnosed and treated early.

Typical clinical signs

Hyperthyroidism is almost exclusively seen in middle- to old-aged cats, and is rarely seen in cats less than seven years of age. Siamese cats seem to have some inherent protection, so suffer less from this condition. The typical signs of hyperthyroidism are increased activity, restlessness, and irritability or clinginess, with an increased appetite but weight loss. Some cats have mild to moderate diarrhoea. Others vomit more than usual Some seem to become super-sensitive to heat and seek out cooler places to sit, and some pant when they are stressed. When the disease is advanced a cat becomes weak and lethargic and loses its appetite. The coat may appear matted or greasy.

Cardiovascular complications

The effect of thyroid hormones on the heart is to stimulate a faster heart rate and a stronger contraction of the heart muscle. Eventually, the muscle of the largest chamber in the heart (the left ventricle) enlarges and thickens as a consequence. This can result in heart failure in untreated cats. Fortunately, once hyperthyroidism has been controlled, the physical changes often improve or resolve completely.

High blood pressure is another common complication and can cause damage to several organs, including the eyes, kidneys, heart, and brain. Following successful treatment for hyperthyroidism,

BRUCE'S KIDNEY TIP

Chronic kidney failure does not occur as a direct effect of hyperthyroidism, but the two diseases often occur together simply because they are both common in older cats. Hyperthyroidism actually increases the blood supply to the kidneys, which can improve their function. When both diseases occur together, it may be in your cat's interest to not treat the hyperthyroidism. Each decision depends on the unique circumstances your cat finds itself in.

the high blood pressure will often spontaneously resolve.

Making a diagnosis

Your vet will examine your cat's neck area for enlarged glands, and check its heart rate and blood pressure.

Most cats with hyperthyroidism have elevated levels of the thyroid hormone T4 in their bloodstream. Both T4 level and routine blood chemistry checks are undertaken, to check how the kidneys are functioning. Because hyperthyroidism either predisposes a cat to, or is associated with, other conditions, the cat's general health is evaluated, especially that of the heart and kidneys.

Prevention and treatment

Because the exact underlying causes of hyperthyroidism aren't known, there are no preventative measures that have yet proved effective. There are three ways to treat hyperthyroidism: through medication, through surgery, or through radioactive-iodine therapy.

Medication

Anti-thyroid drugs, such as methimazole or carbimazole, act by reducing the production of thyroid hormone. These medications provide either short-term control before surgery or, given for life, long-term control of hyperthyroidism.

The drugs are relatively inexpensive, but some cats hate being given tablets. A few cats experience temporary side effects, include vomiting, lethargy, and loss of appetite, but these usually resolve within a few weeks.

Routine blood tests continue during treatment, both to evaluate the effectiveness of the medication and to monitor kidney function.

BRUCE'S SURGERY TIP

Surgical experience with thyroidectomy is vital to avoid inadvertent damage to the parathyroid glands, small glands that lie close to, or within, the thyroid glands themselves. Damage to these glands can result in a life-threatening fall in blood-calcium concentrations. Cats that have had both their thyroid glands removed should be hospitalized for a few days after surgery so that blood-calcium concentrations can be monitored.

Surgical treatment

The surgical removal of the thyroid glands – thyroidectomy – is a relatively straightforward procedure with an excellent success rate.

The advantage of surgery is that it produces a long term or permanent cure in most cats, and eliminates the need for life-long pill giving. To reduce complications, hyperthyroid cats are stabilised with anti-thyroid drugs for several weeks before surgery. Any associated heart disease is also treated.

Radioactive-iodine therapy

Radioactive iodine is administered as a single injection given under the skin. The iodine accumulates in thyroid tissue and destroys it, but does not damage the surrounding tissues or the parathyroid glands. Most treated cats have normal thyroid hormone concentrations restored within three weeks of this safe treatment.

The cat must remain at the facility licensed to use radioactive isotopes until the radiation level has fallen to within acceptable limits, which can be anywhere from two to six weeks. Because of strict treatment guidelines, most facilities don't allow visitors.

Cancers and tumours

A tumour is a collection of abnormal cells that continues to grow and divide without control, usually as growths or lumps. Benign tumours do not spread to other parts of the body or invade surrounding tissues; malignant tumours do have the ability to invade surrounding normal healthy tissue or spread via the bloodstream to other sites in the body. Most of us, when we use the word "cancer", are using it in reference to malignant tumours.

There are many different types of cancer. Carcinomas and sarcomas are solid tumours that arise from various tissues, while lymphomas are solid cancers that originate in white blood cells. Leukemias are immune cell cancers that appear in the blood stream.

Causes of cancer

Just as in us, feline cancers have many different causes, including exposure to sunlight or a wide variety of chemicals. In cats, at least two different viruses, feline leukemia virus (FeLV, see page 135) and feline immunodeficiency virus (FIV, see page 136) can also lead to cancers.

Symptoms and diagnosis

Non-specific changes, such as a poor appetite or lack of energy, or nothing more than weight loss, may be the first indication of an internal cancer. External lumps, wounds that don't heal, or unexplained bleeding are more obvious signs. Although cancer may be a possible diagnosis in older cats, many other diseases commonly cause the same signs.

A diagnosis can sometimes be made through a clinical examination, X-rays, and ultrasound, but an accurate diagnosis can only be made through a microscopic examination of a tissue sample. This is collected through the surgical removal of a small piece of affected tissue, called a biopsy, or by inserting a needle into the tissue and sucking out some cells for microscopic examination, known as a needle aspirate or needle biopsy. Examining a blood sample is routine in the investigation of any suspected cancer. CAT or MRI scans are vital for diagnosing brain tumours or for determining the extent to which a tumour has invaded surrounding tissue.

Lymphoma

Lymphoma, also called malignant lymphoma or lymphosarcoma, is the most common cancer that affects cats. Leukemia, a cancer of the blood or bone marrow, was relatively common in cats when I graduated but it is now, thankfully, quite uncommon. Lymphoma can develop wherever there are white blood cells, usually in lymph nodes anywhere in the body. It often develops at a number of different sites and, in my experience, is the type of cancer most likely to respond to chemotherapy. I have known many cats that, through surgery followed by chemotherapy, went on to have full life expectancies.

Some types of lymphoma are associated with feline leukemia virus (FeLV) infection, but many cats with lymphoma do not have FeLV infection. Generally speaking, lymphoma triggered by FeLV infection tends to occur in younger cats, while lymphoma unrelated to FeLV is more common in older cats. Some cats under two years old develop lymphoma in the chest cavity. Siamese and Oriental breeds are most commonly affected; they often respond very well to treatment and have a good prognosis.

Skin cancer

Squamous cell carcinoma is a skin cancer, and most common in white cats living in sunny climates. This tumour often affects the nose or the ears. At first it may look like a small scratch or wound that doesn't heal well. Fortunately, early treatment of these tumours can be very successful and most commonly involves surgical removal or radiation therapy.

An oral squamous cell carcinoma is much nastier, often invading local bone and spreading to regional lymph nodes. Owners often think that because their cat is drooling saliva or has bad breath that its teeth are to blame. These tumours are frustratingly difficult to cure, although a cat may potentially respond to surgery or radiation therapy.

Breast carcinoma

I still see mammary carcinomas quite frequently in older unneutered females, usually as multiple hard-as-peas lumps in the mammary tissue. Early neutering dramatically reduces the risk of developing this cancer, which can spread to the local lymph nodes and the lungs. Early treatment of small tumours is much more successful than if multiple or larger tumours are present. The most effective treatment is surgical removal of the tumour and associated tissues.

Mast cell tumours

Mast cell tumours commonly affect the skin, the spleen, and the intestines. In the intestines, these are often aggressive tumours that cause blockages. They can be removed surgically, but by the time this is attempted they have spread to lymph nodes, liver, spleen, or lungs. Mast cell tumours affecting the skin can be solitary masses or multiple nodules,

and they sometimes ulcerate. Surgical removal is usually successful, and some mysteriously and spontaneously shrink and disappear with no treatment. Radiation therapy is also useful for some of these tumours.

Fibrosarcoma/soft tissue sarcoma

These cancers form from supporting tissues cells beneath the skin and appear as gradually enlarging, firm masses under the skin. Their degree of malignancy varies enormously. Some are highly malignant, with extensive local invasion of tissues and early spread to lymph nodes and the lungs; others are less aggressive and not so invasive or likely to spread.

In North America, but to a much lesser extent in Europe, soft tissue sarcomas were associated in the 1990s with the injection of rabies vaccine and feline leukemia vaccine. It was then discovered that almost any injection could trigger a soft tissue sarcoma in genetically predisposed cats. Researchers learned that a cold injection triggers more of an inflammatory response than a body-temperature one, and since then I warm vaccines simply by putting the vial in my pocket for five minutes before using it.

Treatment

If a cancer can be surgically eliminated, that is the best option. It is the most likely treatment to result in a cure. Surgery is also used to reduce the bulk of a tumour. It's only when surgery doesn't or can't cure that radiation therapy or chemotherapy should be considered.

Cats tolerate radiation therapy and chemotherapy better than we do, in part because lower doses are sometimes used

Routine preventative health checks are vital for elderly cats because they may appear perfectly normal but have a developing tumour, such as a lymphoma, within.

to avoid side effects that affect the quality of life, and in part because they just seem to be inherently more tolerant.

Maintaining good nutrition is an important part of the care for a cat with cancer. Generally speaking, high quality commercial foods are a good choice, but a cat may also have special dietary needs. Warming food releases its odours and usually encourages the appetite. Sometimes a temporary feeding tube is needed to overcome loss of appetite or an inability to eat. Complete loss of appetite indicates a serious problem such as uncontrolled pain, or side effects from the treatment. Your vet will work with you to try to overcome this.

Old cats act old

Pet cats, particularly those that live only indoors, are living longer than ever before, so it's not surprising that altered behaviour and apparent senility are increasingly common. Sometimes these behaviour changes are caused by organic disease, such as an overactive thyroid gland or a brain tumour. On other occasions, the behaviour change is no more that the consequence of classical behaviour conditioning, such as separation anxiety. But in many instances the reason is true senility. In one study, over a quarter of cats aged 11–14 years old had signs of true senility, and this increased to half of all cats for those aged 15 years or older.

True senility is caused by a combination of reduced blood flow to the brain and chronic free radical damage. Older cats

AGE CALCULATOR

There is no science in this, but we love to compare our cat's age with ours, so use this to compare your cat's age to approximate human equivalents.

1 month	=	10 months
3 months	=	7 years
6 months	=	9 years
1 year	=	24 years
2 years	=	36 years
3 years	=	42 years

and from this point on in steps of three cat years per human year:

4 years	=	45 years
.....		
18 years	=	87 years
19 years	=	90 years
20 years	=	93 years

BRUCE'S SUPPLEMENT TIP

Giving a supplement called Aktivait for two months to older dogs, resulted in significant improvements in signs of disorientation, social interaction, and house soiling. The supplement contains omega-3 fish oils, vitamins E and C, L-carnitine, alpha lipoic acid, coenzyme Q, phosphotidylserine, and selenium. "Aktivait for Cats" is available, although no similar studies on its benefits are presently available. Do not give canine Aktivait to your cat: alpha lipoic acid is toxic to cats.

can develop a hardening of the arteries (arteriosclerosis) and this, together with other medical conditions that cause high blood pressure, anaemia, blood clotting defects, or reduced blood flow, contribute to senile behaviour.

Signs of senility

The signs of senility are subtle, but when combined they are significant. Look for any of the following behaviours.

General behaviour
- A blank expression
- Continuous or repetitive or "stereotyped" pacing
- Lack of grooming, even when age-related pain and disease are controlled

Disorientation
- A delay in recognizing familiar people or places or objects
- Getting lost in familiar surroundings
- Going to the wrong side of a closed door when asking to go through

Changes in sleeping pattern
- Increased daytime sleeping
- Decreased night-time sleeping
- Increased instances of disturbed sleep

Changes in social activities
- Decreased enthusiasm on greeting you
- Decreased speed in response to your requests
- Decreased play with people or with other pets
- Decreased play with other cats
- Increased irritability with anybody or anything
- Failure to complete social interactions

Diagnosing the problem

The medical term for senility, created by a pharmaceutical company, is "cognitive dysfunction" or CD. Because it is a gradual process, treatment of CD is useful and effective, especially in the early stages, but first any associated disease or illness must be controlled. Cats don't complain about pain, but it is a common outrider of old age. Once it is controlled,

FREE RADICAL SCAVENGERS

Oxygen is used by cells to produce energy. A small amount of oxygen is also normally converted within the cell to molecules called "free radicals". As cells age they become less efficient at producing energy, and as a consequence they produce more free radicals. Free radicals are naturally removed by the body's antioxidant defenses. These are called "free radical scavengers" and include special enzymes, the vitamins A, C, and E, and the minerals selenium and zinc. The brain is particularly susceptible to damage from free radicals because it has a high fat content, a high demand for oxygen, and a limited ability to repair itself. If a cat lives long enough, chronic free-radical damage eventually leads to disease processes similar to those seen in humans suffering from senility and Alzheimer's disease.

The outdoors is always stimulating. This golden oldie can still jump up onto a wall and scan the surroundings, both activities that help to delay senile changes.

BRUCE'S LOW-STRESS TIP

Once a cat develops significant clinical signs of senility, any environmental manipulation may actually have a negative effect on its well-being. This is because affected cats often become very stressed and cope poorly with change in their environment, their daily routine, or their diet. If your cat shows signs of stress when you manipulate its environment (not eating, hiding, or changes to toileting habits) return to the former status quo. Some cats may become so upset and cope so poorly with change that they may benefit from being restricted to a single safe room containing everything they need. Synthetic cheek pheromone spray (Feliway, *see* page 121) may be useful.

what was thought to be senility may in fact be reduced activity or mobility because of chronic pain.

There are several licensed pain-killers, especially non-steroid anti-inflammatory drugs (NSAIDs), that have a dramatic effect on reducing pain when used safely. For reasons that simply are not understood, anti-anxiety drugs such as amitryptyline and diazepam may reduce apparent pain in up to 10 per cent of elderly cats. (These drugs do the same in some people. They are not licensed for use in cats.)

Treatment through the environment

Environmental enrichment means nothing more complicated than playing with your cat, talking to it and stroking it, giving it new toys, and laying down food for it to find. Creating a more exciting environment for your cat leads to an increase in nerve growth factors, the growth and survival of more connections between nerve cells, and an increase in brain function – and so less senility.

A five year study feeding healthy older cats a diet supplemented with antioxidants, essential fatty acids, and chicory root (which contains a prebiotic that modifies intestinal flora), resulted in the supplemented cats living significantly longer and more healthily than un-supplemented ones. Most major international cat food manufacturers now produce supplemented diets for older cats, and these may be useful for delaying the onset or progress of CD in cats.

Behaviour changes, even senile behaviour changes, have learned components to them. For example "It hurt when I tried to jump up on the sofa and fell on my back so I won't do that again". Think about what your cat might teach itself.

- Don't change your elderly cat's known environment. Even moving your furniture around is likely to increase its perplexed disorientation.
- Do change your elderly cat's environment, however, to make life easier for it. For example, make a wide, carpeted ramp your cat can walk up to get to its favourite resting or viewing location if it is becoming less agile.
- Introduce (or re-introduce) games such as playing with the ubiquitous feather on a string, in comfortable

surroundings, for example while lying on cushions. Develop a social activity and routine, such as first thing in the morning and again in the afternoon, so that the mental stimulation of playing becomes the learned behaviour.

- Place bits of your cat's favourite food around its home, not too hidden but away from the regular feeding area. This can stimulate an interest in hunting for food.
- Monitor your cat's elimination habits. Provide indoor litter trays for older cats that no longer want to use their previous outdoor lavatory.

Treatment with drugs

As yet, there are no drugs licensed for the treatment of senility in cats. However, a number of drugs have been used "off label". These include selegiline (Selgian), propentofylline (Vivitonin) and nicergoline (Fitergol), all of which have been used in cats with varying degrees of success. The American Association of Feline Practitioners supports the use of selegiline for the treatment of senility in cats. I use propentofylline, as it is unlikely to cause unwanted behavioural side effects. Diazepam (Valium) is also used, but care must be taken because it can damage a cat's liver. Anti-anxiety drugs

---

BRUCE'S BEREAVED CAT TIP

When one cat in a multi-cat family dies, the majority of survivors are affected – but not always as you'd expect. While many search for the departed cat and call more, others literally jump for joy. They become calmer, friendlier, happier. The most sociable, the Siamese and Orientals, are the ones most likely to benefit from the introduction of a new cat.

LOSS OF TOILET TRAINING

Elderly cats that have always used the garden are likely, as the years glide by, to go outside less – either because they don't like the weather or because they no longer want to confront other cats on what was once their own turf. If your outdoor cat messes in your house, it needs an indoor litter tray, now and forever more.

---

such at amytripyline and buspirone are also sometimes used. If the use of any drug is contemplated, ask your vet how much experience she or he has with it in cats.

Older cats groom and play less

Reduced grooming is almost always associated with increased discomfort while grooming. It simply hurts to flex the back enough to clean the anal region, so a cat stops cleaning it. It is too painful to pull out mats, because gums are infected and inflamed and tooth pulp exposed, so a cat stops tidying its hair. Cats are wonderfully programmed to maintain body hygiene, and the majority will do so into old age, but some don't.

Play, more often than not, has to be instigated by you in old age. Some cats stop playing completely, although most elderly cats will still enjoy an occasional play with an activity toy such as a feather on a fishing line.

Treatment

Your vet will diagnose, and when possible treat, the underlying cause of your cat's increasing discomfort. Even with medication to control chronic pain, older cats need your help. Hopefully you trained yours to accept grooming; if so, continue but use a softer brush and take

---

extra care with the comb. The skin is thinner and the backbones are more prominent, especially in skinny cats. Play with your cat but remember, its joints are likely to be arthritic and its ability to focus reduced. Play where you know it is comfortable, for example on your sofa.

Night-time howling and wandering

As hearing diminishes, some cats increase their night-time yowling and wandering. Your vet can check for loss of hearing or an over-active thyroid gland. Any medical condition that increases blood pressure may also be implicated.

More likely, the harsh night-time yowl is a sign of true senility. It is a sign of confusion. Older cats howl more, miaow more, wail more, and seem to learn how to use demand noises more. It's not just the Siamese, although it certainly has the loudest and most wall-piercing voice.

Treatment

To reduce night-time wandering, provide a relatively small and secure area for your cat. The kitchen or your bedroom are both good locations. Place the bed in the warmest spot, for example beside a radiator. If your cat likes feeling enclosed (most do) invert a large cardboard box over the bed, with a cut-out for entering and exiting. Line the bed with sheepskin, synthetic sheepskin such as Vetbed, or thick, insulating thermal fleece. Feed four meals each day, with the last meal just before bedtime. Place the cat in its bed, read its favourite nursery rhyme or whatever makes you feel good, then leave and don't respond to yowling. Your cat

Older cats do slow down. Give them their quiet times, but don't neglect their social side: remember that play can slow both physical and mental decline.

may be senile, but is probably lucid enough to still learn that yowling works. (Take neighbours boxes of chocolates if the yowling penetrates their walls.)

If you are willing to allow your elderly cat the reassurance of being near you at night, in your bedroom, on the bed, then do so. Allowing your cat to sleep with you often dramatically reduces night-time yowling, but don't be surprised if a period of time later – months but perhaps just weeks – it hops off the bed at night, goes elsewhere in the house, and starts yowling again. I've had little success with "brain supplements" in overcoming this condition. Some cat owners use flower essences such as Rescue Remedy. Pragmatically, the occasional use of drugs such as diazepam may be needed, to allow you as well as your cat to get a good night's sleep.

How to make life better for an older cat

- Work out with your vet the best plan for health check-ups.
- Provide at least two indoor litter trays in convenient (for your cat) locations.
- Cover slippery floors with non-slip rugs.
- Feed smaller but more frequent meals, for example four times daily.
- Keep the claws cut: they commonly grow round and into the pads.
- Provide at least two resting beds in comfortable locations. Use insulating fleece for bedding; it retains body heat.
- Play with your golden oldie for a few minutes at least twice daily. A feather on a string is a practical toy.
- Don't get another pet "for the cat". Even if your cat is distressed by the death of a feline companion it may not want another cat in the house.

- The elderly – feline or human – are less comfortable with change than when they (or we) were younger. Stick to routines wherever possible.
- When going on holiday, unless your cat is fully acquainted with a cattery, arrange for your elderly cat to stay at home either with a professional house-sitter or with a reliable friend who visits twice daily.
- If it's a warm and sunny day, take your cat outside. Let it lie on your lap and absorb the sun's rays. That's pure heaven, for both of you.

The end of the road

It's never long enough. The sad fact is that a cat's life is so much shorter than ours. In their later years they cope with the failings of old age with stoicism and natural dignity. They never complain. When they fall, they simply get back up if they can and get on with life. Cats don't look back at what they once could do: they concentrate on here and now, on what they still can do, and they do this remarkably well. But eventually, even the most noble of old timers is no longer able to cope or is living with constant pain. Then it's time to let go.

Decision-making

"Is she suffering?" "Should I keep her going?" "Is it time?" Vets hear these questions every single week. Some of us have developed our own questions to help us give an answer. Is the condition no longer responding to treatment or getting worse? Is there pain or distress that no longer responds to treatment? Is there

Advancing years often lead to reduced mobility due to discomfort, weakness, or poor coordination. This cat must concentrate to walk without falling over.

Even if your elderly cat is comfortable, safe, and well fed, more often than not, you will have to decide when its quality of life drops below an acceptable minimum.

permanent lost of vital body functions that cannot be restored? Has old age wear and tear permanently affected the cat's quality of life?

Euthanasia is simple

When the time comes, a concentrated anaesthetic is simply given intravenously. Some owners think their cats know what's happening, but they don't. All a cat knows is that someone holds a leg – something that's happened before when a blood sample was taken or a medicine given intravenously – and then comes a feeling of sleepiness. Your cat loses consciousness, and within a few seconds the heart stops. Brain death occurs within a few more seconds, but electrical activity in muscles can last for up to ten minutes, causing twitches. If the respiratory muscles are affected there can be a reflex contraction of the diaphragm, producing a "gasp" as if the cat were still alive. It isn't.

Grieving is complicated

The intensity of loss can catch us out. A few weeks after one of my pets died, talking to Japanese vets about pet loss, I choked up and couldn't speak for over a minute. I felt like a fool.

Grief can be frightening and sometimes uncontrollable. It doesn't follow any set pattern, but most of us go through a series of feelings: numbness, yearning, despair, and then acceptance and with time, resolution. It can disrupt daily life. It can be complicated, especially if you have other unresolved losses where you were unable to express your feelings or had little social support. Both sudden

deaths and those that occur after long illnesses can lead to complicated grief. But remember, grieving is normal.

Grieving eventually resolves

There is no magic pill that can remove the pain completely but with time the feelings become less intense.

Don't beat yourself up over the way you feel. When someone tells me "I can't believe that losing a cat would wreck my entire life!" I try to remind them not to feel ashamed about having such strong feelings, not to apologise about the way they feel, and never to chastise themselves for it. For many of us, our pets really are that important.

If your cat is seriously ill, you may even start grieving before it dies, and the death itself can actually bring about a feeling of relief. This is particularly the case with a long and difficult illness, although it doesn't mean you feel less pain when the actual death occurs.

The new cat in your life

Life and death. Love and grief. There's always the other side, but for most of us tears inevitably give way to smiles, to fond memories. The right time for another cat is when you know it's the right time. If you've read through this book, I know what type of person you are and also know there's a lucky cat somewhere out there waiting for you to become its personal staff.

A GOOD DEATH

Euthanasia means voluntarily ending the life of an individual who's suffering from a terminal illness or other incurable condition. The word comes from the Greek words "eu" meaning good and "thanatos" meaning death. For those who have watched a cat quickly fall asleep and then seconds later seen his or her heart stop, the procedure is aptly named.

INDEX

Figures in *italics* indicate captions.

ACKNOWLEDGEMENTS

Let me apologise for repeating myself but I still can't quite believe I've been in veterinary practice, examining cats and dogs and a few other species, for over forty years. Translate that into numbers and I've carried out somewhere between fifty and one hundred thousand clinical examinations and operations. So, first of all, thanks, cats! I knew little about felines when I graduated; medically speaking cats didn't count in the 1960s. If I know any more now than I did then, it's because of all those daily encounters, with cats but also with their people.

As always, those I work with at the London Veterinary Clinic all fill in (or say "thank goodness") on the days I take off work to write. Thanks to my fellow vets, Veronica Aksmanovic, Philippa Mitchell and Grant Petrie and the best veterinary nurses anywhere, Ashley McManus, Suzi Gray, Hester Small, Letty Lean and Angela Bettinson for all your help and your experience with cats. Appreciation too, to everyone at MB, publisher David Lamb, who commissioned the book and let me write what I think rather than only what's anodyne, Helen Griffin the commissioning editor and Georgina Atsiaris the always cheerful, always efficient project editor. Thanks to the art editor, Juliette Norsworthy who consistently produces clean, clear and attractive pages, and to Joanne Wilson who helped the project to completion.

And finally, my gratitude to copy editor Candida Frith-Macdonald. The copy editor is the person a writer – certainly this writer – relies on most. And once you work with one who understands how you think, it's magic. Thanks magician.

Governing Council of the Cat Fancy
5 King's Castle Business Park,,
The Drove, Bridgwater
Somerset, TA6 4AG, UK
+44 (0)1278 427575
www.gccfcats.org

The Fédération Internationale Féline (FIFE),
17 Rue du Verger, L-2665 Luxembourg
fifeweb.org

Felis Britannica -FB (UK FIFE representatives), 21 Buckingham Avenue, Cheltenham, Gloucestershire,
GL51 8DA
+44 (0)1242 238228
www.felisbritannica.co.uk

The International Cat Association (TICA)
PO Box 2684, Harlingen
Texas 78551
+1 (956) 428-8046

www.tica.org
www.tica-uk.org.uk

The Cat Fanciers' Association, Inc.
1805 Atlantic Avenue, Manasquan
NJ 08736
+1 (732) 528-9797
www.cfa.org

Welfare organizations

Blue Cross, Shilton Road,
Burford, Oxfordshire
OX18 4PF
+44 (0)1993 822651
www.bluecross.org.uk

Cats Protection
National Cat Centre
Chelwood Gate, Sussex
RH17 7TT
+44 (0)8707 708649
www.cats.org.uk

The People's Dispensary for Sick Animals (PDSA)
Whitechapel Way, Priorslee,
Telford, Shropshire
TF2 9PQ
+44 (0)1952 290999
www.pdsa.org.uk

Wood Green Animal Shelters
www.woodgreen.org.uk

Further information
Feline Advisory Bureau (FAB)
Taeselbury, High Street
Tisbury, Wiltshire
SP3 6LD
United Kingdom
+44 (0)1747 871 872
www.fabcats.org

Pets Travel Scheme
ww2.defra.gov.uk (under "Wildlife and Pets")

Breeds, myths, history, welfare
www.messybeast.com

Cat foods
Almo: www.almonature.eu
Applaws: www.mpmproducts.co.uk
Burns: www.burnspet.co.uk
Arden Grange: www.ardengrange.com
Felix: www.catslikefelix.co.uk
Go-Cat: www.go-cat.co.uk
Hill's: www.hillspet.co.uk
IAMS: www.iams.co.uk
James Wellbeloved: www.wellbeloved.com
Orijen: www.orijenpetfoods.co.uk
Purina: www.purinaone.co.uk
Royal Canin: www.royalcanin.co.uk
Sheba: www.uk.sheba.com
Whiskas: www.whiskas.co.uk

Photographic acknowledgements

akg-images blickwinkel/PICANI/S Klewitz-Seemann 50 b

Alamy Andre Jenny 16 a; Arco Images GmbH/C Steimer 157 ar; Art Directors & TRIP/Helene Rogers 112, 143 a; CaptureIt 153 r; Caro/Oberhaeuser 75; F Vrouenraths (Kenia) 151 bl; Graphic Science 138 r; Horizon International Images Limited 94 a; Ian Middleton 116; imagebroker/Michael Weber 90 a; Jenny Tonkin Nature Images 154; Johner Images/Peter Carlsson 25; Julie Woodhouse 86 b; Juniors Bildarchiv 17 b, 26 bl & br, 31 b, 129, 135 l, 151 al, 170; Keith Mindham 159; Mark Scheuern 37 r; Natalya Onishchenko 28-9; O Digoit 108; Papilio/Robert Pickett 153 l; Patty Harry 87 a; petographer 25 b, 131 b; Petra Wegner 151 ac & ar; Richard Sheppard 149; Rodger Tamblyn 56 b, 85 r; Steppenwolf 178; tbkmedia.de 24; The Art Archive/Gianni Dagli Orti 15 r; Tierfotoagentur/R Richter 34a, 39; Top-Pics TBK 12; Wildlife GmbH 174; Wildscape/ajs 183

Ardea Jean Michel Labat 87 b, 187; John Daniels 110, 130, 186

Corbis Beateworks/Dana Hoff 9; Benjamin

Rondel/First Light 134; Janie Airey/cultura 59 a

Dorling Kindersley 109; Gary Ombler 161 a

Dreamstime.com 65; Garya 46 a; Jolita 58 a; Pazo 84 al

Fotolia aceshot 86 a; Alena Ozerova 171; Aliaksei Lasevich 69; amelie 81; Andrejs Pidjass 132-3; Andrey Stratilatov 78 b; Anobis 22 a, 33; Bartlomiej Nowak 50 a; biglama 25 a, 64 a; calamity john 54 br; Callalloo Candcy 42 b, 47 b, 54 bl, 55 b, 67; Callalloo Twisty 21 b; Callalloo Alexis 43; Callalloo Fred 45; Carmen Steiner 91; Christiane Robin 31 a; contrastwerkstatt 161 b; diefotomacher 137; dimch 84 cr; Dixi 38 r; Dmitry Naumov 47 a; EcoView 14; emprise 44 l; Enrico Scarsi 7; epantha 27 ar; Eric Gevaert 56 a; Eric Isselée 8, 30 bl, 32 a, 38 l, 52 a, 80 b; Esme7 32 b; Fortish 84 ar; galbertone 96; Galló Gusztáv 82; haveseen 76; HelleM 54 ar; hosphotos 74; Igor Korionov 2; Igor Zhorov 70; Igors Leonovs 42 a; Inferna 30 a, 63 b, 168; ixusfan 58 b; Jazavac 68; Johanna Goodyear 73 b; Julia Vadi 23 a; Katerina Cherkashina 52 a; kathy libby 59 b; kazoka303030 78 a; Kelpfish 83 b; Kirill Vorobyev 36, 117;

Krissi Lundgren 26 a, 34 b, 63 a; Laurent Dambies 57 b; MAErtek 10-11; Maksym Dyachenko 57 ar; Marcin Sadlowski 53; Maria Sauh 150; Marilyn Barbone 57 al; Marina Moskovich 21 a; Mark Bond 172; Maruba 84 cl; Max Tactic 114; Mega 41 b; Michael Pettigrew 84 b; Michael Ransburg 79 a; Mknace 163; Monkey Business 142; Mr Flibble 145; Nadine Haase 131 a; NatUlrich 100 b; NiDerLander 139; Olga Struk 124; Oscar Williams 165; Parrus 79 b; Patricia Hofmeester 80 a; Paweł Syrjus 44 r; Renee McCrady 143 br; Ruth Black 72; Sebastien Montier 64 b; Shakzu 83 al & ar; Simone van den Berg 20 a, 71; Sunshine Photos 173; Svetoslav Radkov 73 a; Thomas Launois 136; Tony Campbell 62; tsach 41 a; Valery Vasiliev 46 b; Zimon 55 a; ZTS 77

Getty Images FotoFealing 88-9; Michael Blann 121; Steve Lyne 85 l

Helmi Flick 19

Mary Evans Picture Library 40 b

Nature Picture Library Jane Burton 66

Octopus Publishing Group Adrian Pope 99; Ray Moller 16b, 17 a, 18 a, bl & br, 20 b, 22 b, 23 b, 27 al & b, 30 br, 31 c, 40 a

Photolibrary Group Aflo Foto Agency/ Shuji Aizawa & Kyoko Aizawa 177; age fotostock/Carrie Villines 120; Animals Animals/James Robinson 141 b; BSIP Medical/Oliel 93 r, /Hanet 181; Garden Picture Library/Gert Tabak 169; HillCreek Pictures BV 106-7; imagebroker/Konrad Wothe 54 al, /Sonja Krebs 126 l; Juniors Bildarchiv 37 l, 51, 92, 93 l, 94 b, 97, 98, 99 b, 100 a, 111, 118, 122, 123, 127, 143 bl, 144, 148, 152, 156, 157 al, 162 a; Mauritius/ Klaus Scholz 135 r, /Nelly Ampersand 147; MIXA Co Ltd 48-9; Nordic Photos/Anna G Tufvesson 119; Oxford Scientific/Alain Christof 95, /Les Stocker 90 b, /London Scientific Films 141 a; Superstock/Yoshio Tomii 60-1; Vstock, LLC 185

Rex Features 166; Phil Yeomans 35

RSPCA Photolibrary Angela Hampton 151 br, 162 b

Science Photo Library Tom Myers 138 l

StickyPaws® 126 r

The Art Archive Eileen Tweedy 15 l

Warren Photographic Jane Burton 155, 157 bl & br, 158, 160